Some Observations on Salmon and Trout
Frederick M. Chamberlain

Publisher's Note

The book descriptions we ask booksellers to display prominently warn that this is an historic book with numerous typos or missing text; it is not indexed or illustrated.

The book was created using optical character recognition software. The software is 99 percent accurate if the book is in good condition. However, we do understand that even one percent can be an annoying number of typos! And sometimes all or part of a page may be missing from our copy of the book. Or the paper may be so discolored from age that it is difficult to read. We apologize and gratefully acknowledge Google's assistance.

After we re-typeset and design a book, the page numbers change so the old index and table of contents no longer work. Therefore, we often remove them; otherwise, please ignore them.

Our books sell so few copies that you would have to pay hundreds of dollars to cover the cost of our proof reading and fixing the typos, missing text and index. Instead we let most customers download a free copy of the original typo-free scanned book. Simply enter the barcode number from the back cover of the paperback in the Free Book form at www.RareBooksClub.com. You may also qualify for a free trial membership in our book club to download up to four books for free. Simply enter the barcode number from the back cover onto the membership form on our home page. The book club entitles you to select from more than a million books at no additional charge. Simply enter the title or subject onto the search form to find the books.

If you have any questions, could you please be so kind as to consult our Frequently Asked Questions page at www.RareBooksClub.com/faqs.cfm? You are also welcome to contact us there.

General Books LLC™, Memphis, USA, 2012. ISBN: 9781151367143.

❧❧❧❧❧❧❧❧

DEPARTMENT OF COMMERCE AND LABOR BUREAU OF FISHERIES GEORGE M. BOWERS, Comm1ss1oaer SOME OBSERVATIONS ON SALMON AND TROUT IN ALASKA. By F. M. Chamberlain, *Naturalist, U.S. Fisheries Steamer Albatross.*

Bureau of Fisheries Document No. 627.
CONTENTS.
rip.
Introduction
Distinctive characters of the species »
Common names »
Differentiating marks in adults »
Designations of young salmon
Hybridization 10
Resemblance of the young 11
Detailed descriptions of the young 13
Humpback salmon 1
Dog salmon 14
King salmon 16
Coho salmon 18
Sockeye salmon"
Steelhead trout 19
Charr, or Dolly Varden trout 19
The basins studied 20
Conditions controlling the work 20
Method used to determine migratory movements 21
The Naha 22
Character of the stream 22
Yield of salmon 23
Catch of young salmon in the trap 26
Yes Bay Stream 27
Karluk River 28
Suitability as a spawning stream 28
Movements of young salmon as shown by trial catches 28
Conditions reported in British Columbia 30
Summary of observations 31
Young salmon in fresh water 31
The sockeye 31
Movement of fry above the lakes 31
Food and feeding 32
Food supply in relation to the hatching season 34
Growth in fresh water 34
Migration of yearlings 36
King salmon 40
Age and season of migration 40
Effect of change from fresh to salt water 42
Food 43
Coho salmon 44
Earliest migrations 44
Food and habits 44

3

Young salmon in fresh water—Continued. Pa8R
Dog Balmon.' 47
Humpback salmon 48
Trout and charr 48
Sea habits of young salmon 50
Notes afforded by collections and records 50
The sockeye 50
King salmon; 53
Coho 53
Dog and humpback salmon 55
Conclusions from available data 57
Abundance of food 57
Return of adults to fresh water 59
Approach of schools, 60
Food and feeding 61
The sockeye 61
King salmon 64
Coho 64
Humpback and dog salmon 65
Relation of food supply to number of adult salmon 65
Age of adult salmon 66
Salmon-marking experiments 66
Methods 66
Regeneration of lost parts 67
Salmon in the Trocadero, at Paris 68
Factors influencing return to fresh water 69
Sex instincts versus condition of nutrition 69
The different runs 70
Temperature 71
Currents 73
Ascent of streams 74
Interval between arrival and spawn-

ing 75
  Parent streams 76
  "Introduction into streams not previously frequented" 77
  "Return of marked salmon" 78
  "Distinctive and characteristic runs" 78
  Variations in weights and measurements 79
  Variations in counts 89
  Streams not utilized by sockeyes 92
  Relation of size of run to spawning area 93
  Selection of spawning ground 94
  Conditions required by the sockeye 94
  Preferences of the king salmon 96
  Spawning streams chosen by the coho, dog. and humpback salmon... 97
  Nature of spawning beds selected 98
  Deposit of eggs. 99
  Completeness of spawning 160
  Percentage of natural production 101
  Relation of spawning habits to number of fish 102
  Changes incident to maturation 104
  Return of adults to salt water 106
  Enemies of young salmon 107
  Geographical glossary 109

I SOME OBSERVATIONS ON SALMON AND TROUT IN ALASKA, By F. M. Chamberla1n,
Naturalist, U. S. Fisheries Steamer Albatross.

INTRODUCTION.

To assist in the solution of various problems, it was deemed desirable in connection with the Alaska salmon investigation of 1903 to establish shore stations. The work at these stations was to comprise not only the study of the habits of the salmon in fresh waters and adjacent bays, but, in addition, a reconnaissance of all the neighboring basins with reference to available hatchery sites, observation of the methods employed in taking fish for the canneries, an inquiry into the sea habitat and the factors influencing the return of the adult fish, an inquiry into the efficiency of the hatcheries then operated, and a general study of the biological features of territory immediately adjacent to the stations. The facilities offered by the establishments of the Alaska Packers' Association at Loring and at Karluk determined the adoption of the Naha and Karluk rivers as localities for this work. "

The greater part of the data obtained at these shore stations is contained in unpublished reports. In the present paper are presented such of the facts as bear upon the natural history of the salmon and, with a view to the application of these results in future work, some notes on the methods used in the inquiry. Most of the material contained herein relates to young salmon, but the known facts in the life of the adult, including the spawning period, are considered, and mention is made also of the trout as associated with the salmon. A chapter differentiating and describing the species, particularly in the finger a The observations in the latter region were made between the early part of May and September, 1903, by the late Cloudsley Rutter, naturalist of the steamer *Albatross,* assisted by M. H. Spaulding, of Stanford University. At Loring the work was carried on during 1903 and 1904 in charge of the writer, assisted at different times by E. L. Goldsborough and H. D. Aller, of the Bureau of Fisheries, and H. C. Fassett, fishery expert on the steamer *Albatross.* During the summer of 1905 observations along some of the above lines were continued by the writer at Yes Bay, in connection with other work of the.4Z&aross, with the assistance of Mr. Fassettandof J. S. Burcham,of Stanford University.
6 ling stage, is followed by a detailed record of the field observations on the young, and upon these data, which are largely statistical, is based the succeeding discussion of the habits of the salmon from the time of the migration of the young until the return of the adults to the spawning beds. Liberal use has been made in this discussion of the results of previous workers on the subject, and, in addition to the collections and notes made by the shore parties in Alaska in 1903, 1904, and 1905, all of the *Albatross* collections of young salmon now in possession of the Bureau have been studied. The concluding chapters of the report are given to the discussion of questions relating to the adult salmon, and contain in tabular form the statistics of weights and measurements of nearly 10,000 sockeye salmon, with anatomical counts of about 4,600 of these. In the entire paper the sockeye, as the most valuable commercial salmon of Alaska, has been made the main feature. DISTINCTIVE CHARACTERS OF THE SPECIES. COMMON NAMES.

The most common appellations of the various species as they are known in Alaska are used in this paper. There seems to be no reason why, for example, the words "quinnat," "chinook," and "king," which in a loose way pertain, respectively, to the Sacramento, Columbia, and Alaskan *tschawytscha,* should be continued to the confusion of readers. The "blueback" of the Columbia differs in no specific essential from the "sockeye" of Alaska. Names based on characters common to several species, such as "red," "silver," etc., are especially apt to be confusing. The name "trout" as here applied to small fingerlings may include steelhead, rainbow, and cutthroat. Individual variations in both trout and salmon overlap the limiting points in most characters, but in the salmon the sum of various characters sets the five American species distinctly apart. Careful examination has so far failed to show any distinguishing character to differentiate the young of these trouts. Indeed, apparently no specific difference is constant in the adult.

DIFFERENTIATING MARKS IN ADULTS.
Fishermen and large handlers of salmon roughly but very accurately distinguish the adults of different species by certain obvious characters. The king salmon is known by the small black spots on the tail. The tail of the humpback is spotted, but with larger oblong spots. The backs of both king and coho are commonly spotted, the spots of the coho being as a rule smaller than those of the king, but these spots are not noted by fishermen. Rarely the sockeye shows a few spots, particularly on the tail, but these are never distinct as in the other species.

(To the sea-run form only does this statement apply; the dwarf lake-dweller is spotted.) The steelhead, also a spotted fish, is at once recognized by its slimness, the square tail fin, and the deep caudal peduncle. It is difficult to pick up a steelhead by grasping the tail, whereas a salmon may be readily so held. Salmon without spots—sockeye, dog salmon, and sometimes the coho— are somewhat confusing. The sockeye is usually distinguishable by the blue back after death, the sharp nose, and the narrow maxillary, while the tail fin lacks the produced pointed lobes of the dog salmon; also the scales are firmer and show a clean-cut paving, and the flesh is intensely red. The coho and dog salmon scales when silvery appear to be of a finer and more delicate texture than those of the sockeye. This is especially notable in the dog salmon. The female dog salmon is usually very deep, both dorsoventrally and in lateral thickness— "plumpness." The caudal peduncle is less compressed than in other species and the curves joining it to the body are shorter than in the coho. In the Alaska fisheries the dog-salmon males are seldom taken until the secondary sex characters begin to be developed—the "hookbill" and dirty coloration." The produced caudal rays mentioned above and the light color of the flesh are distinguishing marks in this species. The coho is distinguished from the dog by less delicate scales and deeper peduncle, by its small pupil, and in general by the occurrence of spots often at first overlooked.

In closer examination one will consider the greater length and fineness of the gillrakers in the sockeye, the increased number of anal and branchiostegal rays in the king, the fine scales of the humpback, the large and few pyloric cceca of the coho. The dog salmon possesses no single diagnostic mark, but differs from the other species respectively in each character as mentioned above. Changes incidental to the spawning period will be noted under that head.

DESIGNATIONS OF YOUNG SALMON.

The lack of a distinctive terminology for the young of fishes has led to much confusion in the interpretation of reports of fish culturists and investigators, more or less consequent acrimonious debate, and some legal entanglements. In an effort to settle this matter for the benefit of American writers and readers, the American Fisheries Society in 1905 adopted the following nomenclature:6 *FYy=6ak* up to the time the yolk sac is absorbed and feeding begins.

Advanced fry=fish from the end of the fry period until they have reached a length of 1 inch. *Fingerling8=fish.* between the length of 1 inch and the yearling stage, the various sizes to be designated as follows: No. 1, a fish 1 inch in length and up to 2 inches; "" In11andling a large number of dog salmon in 1907 it was observed at Juneau early in September that many green silvery males were being taken in the traps at Shelter Island and vicinity. Among these were several dog-salmon grilse." (Fassett.) 6 Report of the Commissioner of Fisheries for fiscal year ended June 30, 1906, p. 24. no. 2, a fish 2 inches in length and up to 3 inches; no. 3, a fish 3 inches in length and up to 4 inches, etc. *Yearlings=G&h* that are 1 year old, but less than 2 years old from the date of hatching. These may be designated no. 1, no. 2, no. 3, etc., after the plan described for fingerlings.

These definitions have been generally adopted in government and state reports and are the ones used in this paper. The use of the French term "alevin" instead of "fry" for the larval stage of salmonids has been abandoned here for the reason that the French writers do not restrict the term to that period of development of the young fish. Though the use of "alevin" has had the support of such authorities as Francis Day", Livingston Stone6, and Cloudsley Rutter0, it seems unnecessary, if not even absurd, to continue the use of a foreign word and give it a meaning not recognized in the language, from which it is drawn, more especially as even the writers mentioned above did not make a strict application of the term.

Some French writersd have apparently endeavored to make a technical use of the terms "alevin" and "fretin," but their example has not been followed by later writers, and the word alevin seems to b'e used now to designate the young of the salmon in the most general way. 4 In the same manner the German word "Brut," or "Jungbrut," has about the same latitude as has been given hitherto to the word " fry" in English, nor does the German term "Setzlinge" admit of strict application/

The words "larva" and "larval" have been used by many writers in descriptions of the young salmonids. Others would restrict these terms to fishes exhibiting a greater change in the stages, such as the eels and the ladyfish. As in neither case is there a complete metamorphosis, this limitation is scarcely tenable. The terms, however, are not yet current among fish culturists.

The great diversity of size among species and among individuals of a given species at the time of hatching, as well as the intimate dependence of fish growth upon environment, in some cases may

"Francis Day, British and Irish Salmonidce, p. 43, 44, and 82, 1887. 6 Livingston Stone, Domesticated trout, p. 151, 6th ed., 1901.
c Cloudsley Rutter, Natural history of the quinnat salmon, Bulletin U. S. Fish Commission, vol. Xx11, 1902, p. 69 and 72. *d* Larbaletrier, Albert, Traite-Manuel de Pisciculture d'eau douce, p. 220, 1886: "Alevins.—Les jeunes poissons vcnant d'eclore portent le nom *d'alevins.* Toutefois, il est a remarquer que cette denomination s'applique surtout aux jeunes dessaumons, truites et ombres-chevalier, tant qu'ils n'ont pas r6sorbe la vesicule; apres, ils constituent le *fretin;* pour les carpes et autres cyprins, quelques auteurs prferent l'appellation de *feuilles.* Cette distinction ne nous semble pas necessaire; d'ailleurs, nous ne sommes pas seul a penser de la sorte, car le nom d'alevin tend a se generalises"
« C. Raveret-Wattel, La Pisciculture, vol. u, 1907, p. 185.
/Paul Vogel, Ausfiihrliches Lehrbuch der Teichwirthschaft, p. 334, 341, 347, 349, 1898. seem to introduce inconsis-

tency into the definitions adopted. Thus under some circumstances a yearling charr might be found of less size than a salmon fry; but it is believed that by use of the above nomenclature an exact interpretation of language will always be made possible. As in all instances involving individual characters, physiological and physical limits may overlap. Salmon fry usually begin to feed before the complete absorption of the yolk, a remnant of the yolk being persistent even for some time after the ventral walls have united and all outward appearance of the sac has been lost; and hence the migrating young of the salmon could with equal propriety be termed fry, since many still have yolk remnants, or fingerlings, since they have begun to a small degree to feed and have become over an inch in length. In this paper, in all cases where the schools contain many individuals with the embryonic fin membrane still evident, the term "fry" is retained. In case of the humpback and dog salmon young which were taken in salt water, it is sometimes impossible to know whether "fingerling" or "yearling" is the proper designation, but since it seems probable that the greater number were less than one year of age, the term "fingerling" is used. In the case of the coho the distinction is even more doubtful, but is applied with as much discrimination as the state of our knowledge permits.

The terms "parr" and "grilse" have come into American use from the British writers on Salmonidse, but the latter designation has attained a meaning somewhat different from the original.

"Grilse," as applied to the Atlantic salmon *(Salmo solar)* by both American and British writers, refers to the incompletely grown fish which return from the sea to the rivers to spawn. Unlike the Pacific salmon *(Oncorhynchus)*, the Atlantic salmon, both male and female, mature perfect sex products before completing their growth, and after spawning in the same manner as the grown fish of one or more years' greater age, return to the sea as "grilse-kelts" to cont inue their growth and return the following season (or second year after) as "salmon." What are known as "grilse" among Pacific salmon are the small males, presumably lacking at least one year of the usual age of adults of the species, which leave the sea for the spawning beds, mature perfect milt, but after "spawning" die in the same manner as fully grown males. Females in no instance show this precocity. While there are sometimes small females among mature fish, they grade into the regular size in such manner that they can only be supposed to be those individuals which by heredity or unfavorable environment have failed by a greater or less degree to reach the standard size. (See p. 86-87.)

The term "parr" is applied in general to young fish still in fresh water and showing the dark bars or parr marks. They may be fingerlings, or yearlings, or even adults. The males of this stage in the case of the Pacific salmon in some instances mature perfect spermatozoa, but whether they spawn and die immediately afterwards is not known, nor is it known definitely whether fingerling parrs may develop the sex product.

The terms "smolt" (frequently still spelled and pronounced "smelt") and "kelt" as used for stages of the Atlantic salmon hardly have parallels in the case of the Pacific salmon. If any of the genus *Oncorhynchus* return to sea as kelts, it has not yet been fully demonstrated, and almost the entire weight of evidence is against the belief that it ever occurs. The term "smolt" (French "tacon") is applied, in contradistinction to parr, to that stage of *Salmo salar* when, in fresh water, the parr marks are lost and the young fish assumes its livery of silver in preparation for its descent to the sea." It might be used with some propriety of the yearling migrating sockeye, but it seems undesirable to confuse further the meaning of words which have their proper use only with the eastern species.

HYBRIDIZATION.

The question of natural hybridization has never been investigated, though it has long been well known that trout may be artificially crossed and fertile hybrids produced.6 That the species of salmon may be variously crossed with success has also been demonstrated, but owing to the difficulty of retaining them in fresh water until of breeding age the fertility of salmon hybrids has not been proved. Rarely adult salmon are taken which seem to possess characters of two species, but on the basis of predominating characters they have been assigned to one or the other of the species and the possibility of a hybrid ignored. The differences in time and place selected, by the different, species of salmon for spawning minimizes the possibility of natural hybridization; and the deficient vitality of crossed eggs and hybrid fry is, perhaps, sufficient to account for the failure of most if not all such accidental product when natural vicissitudes must be overcome. Moreover, the young of the different species of salmon are distinct and show characteristically distinct habits. This is not so evident, however, in Alaskan trout. Rainbows and steelheads spawn together in the Naha. Spawning cutthroats have not been noted there because they do not happen to inhabit that portion of the Naha which was under observation; but their segregation is inconstant. One species or the other may be most numerous in the lower or upper reaches of a stream. In the Naha basin cutthroats are more numerous Day, op. cit., p. 90.

6 For a full discussion of hybridization of trout, see "British and Irish Salmonidse" by Francis Day, p. 47-60, 254-270, pi. x and xi, 1887, and Paul Vogel, op, cit., p. 308, 311. in the upper sections of the system; at Yes Bay the case is reversed. If the fry and fingerlings of the three recognized species possess any distinctive marks or habits these have so far escaped detection. RESEMBLANCE OF THE YOUNG.

By one who knows the adult salmon, the young of the salmon are not apt to be confused with any fishes except trout. Of the fishes having an adipose dorsal they are readily distinguishable from the capelin, smelt, and eulachon by the siphon-shaped stomach and numerous ccecal appendages; the grayling is known by its high dorsal fin; the whitefish by its comparatively small mouth.

The young of the true trout very greatly resemble the spotted species of salmon, and are distinguishable mainly by the short anal fin. The salmons usually show at least 14 fully developed—that is, full length—rays, exclusive of the 3 to 5 short, simple (unbranched) rays in the front of the fin. Sometimes there are but 13, and in rare instances only 12, while the number may be increased to 17 in the sockeye, which normally has 14, and in the king salmon, with 16 as a normal, the extreme will doubtless be still greater. The trout have normally 10 to 12 developed rays in the anal, but while this seems little separated from the number given for the salmon, as a rule the extra length of the fin in the latter may be noted by even a casual comparison. When spread the fin of the trout fingerling shows a rounded outline, the front rays somewhat more evenly graduated than in the salmon and the hinder rays much higher in proportion, causing it to resemble the dorsal in general outline. The anal of the salmon fingerling usually has a slightly concave outer margin, the hinder rays being shortened. The charr (Dolly Varden, or "salmon trout"), in addition to the characters of the anal as just described for the true trout, is distinguishable by the peculiarly mottled coloration, and in the advanced stages also by the less compressed body.

The different species of salmon *Oncorhynchus)* are not usually difficult to distinguish from one another, yet individual variations sometimes confuse the determination. While in adults the sum of various differentiating characters makes it possible to decide the species, the late development of some characters greatly increases the problem in immature examples. It is possible that some local variations obtain; for example, sockeye fingerlings from Wood River seem to have a much smaller eye than fingerlings of the same size and species in Southeast Alaska. There is also much variation in the length and number of gillrakers in the young of this species and perhaps also in those of the humpback salmon. From the number of specimens at present available for study it can not be determined whether or not this variation is of geographical origin.

The humpback *(O. gorbuscha)* is unique among the salmons in never developing the parr marks. It is usually entirely silvery in all the young stages, and is the only one of the salmons whose young up to some 6 inches in length, taken in fresh water, will show no parr marks even under the scales. As possible exceptions to this must be noted the dwarf sockeye, whose young are as yet unknown, and perhaps small mature fishes returning for spawning.

The fingerlings of the dog salmon *(0. Tceta)* have the parr marks sometimes much reduced, and those readily disappear in poorly preserved specimens. But where several examples are at hand the greater average size in the younger stages, the slightly different outline, and the presence of these marks will always distinguish them from the humpback.

Of the four species of strongly marked fingerlings the steelhead *(Salmo gairdneri)* may be recognized by its short anal, as noted above for trout, and by its small size taken at the season of migration. The sockeye *(O. nerka),* king *(O. tschawytscha),* and coho *(O. Icisutch),* being all for some time resident in fresh water and hence very variable in size, require close inspection for trustworthy identification. In general, in the fingerling stage the sockeye will be recognized by its more slender and tapering form, and by the more nearly circular outline of the parr marks, though this latter does not always hold true. The coho is usually distinguishable by the orange tints of the lower fins (a character rarely absent) and by the white front margins of both anal and dorsal, but especially by the falcation of the anal through the extreme production or elongation of the first developed rays. The king, very similar to the coho in general outline, does not exhibit this extreme form of the anal, and in the specimens examined from the Karluk River the parr marks are larger and the marking of the back much more notable. In a careful examination the sockeye can almost always be identified by the greater length and number of the gillrakers, and the king by the greater number of branchiostegal and anal fin rays. (See detailed descriptions following.)

In salt water the parr marks are rapidly covered by the brilliancy of the silver, so that, except the king and coho, which are spotted, all the species soon become plain. It is not known when the spots of the adult humpback first appear. Whether this obliteration of the parr marks by the silver overcast is caused by the salt water may be questioned, although in the trout, which are known to run indifferently in salt and fresh water, the change is marked, fish from salt water being much more silvery. I have taken one example of sockeye yearling in Jordan Lake that seems almost as silvery as the salt-water individuals of the same size, but it is entirely unlikely that it had returned from the sea."

"See under suiolt, p. 10. Day, op. cit., p. 90,

Another change with residence in the sea is a rapid increase in proportional depth. This is most marked in the coho. Seven examples from the head of Naha Bay, May 31, length 98 to 117 mm., had depth 4.6 to 5, while in four examples taken August 2, at the cannery wharf, 154 to 210 mm. length, the depth is 3.75 to 4.4, which approaches the normal depth of the adult fish with matured sex products (3.5 to 4 +).

DETAILED DESCRIPTIONS OF THE YOUNG.

The following key will assist in the identification of small fingerlings. In larger examples—as large fingerlings and yearlings—the specific characters of the adult must be the main reliance.

Key For Identiflcation Of Young Salmon And Trout Between 1 And 2 Inches

In Length.

With adipose lin, large mouth, moderate dorsal fin, siphon-shaped stomach,
a. Anal fin long, at least 12 developed rays, the last of these much shorter than the first, giving the fin a straight or concave margin or outline Salmon. b.

Showing no distinct parr marks. Back dark in dead examples *gorbuscha*. bb. Usually with distinct parr marks.
c. Parr marks less distinct, mainly above lateral line, body comparatively slender; gillrakers short, equal to less than 2 interspaces; eye small. *Tceta*. cc. Parr marks more distinct, showing below lateral line; body rather slender or deep; eye large,
d. Gillrakers long, equal to or greater than 2 interspaces; body rather slender; parr marks tending to become circular *nerka*. dd. Gillrakers short; body deep; parr marks well defined bars. e. Parr marks narrower than interspaces, often orange coloration on fins; brancbiostegals and anal rays few, 13 or 14; anal with marginal stripes *hisutch*. ee. Parr marks wider than interspaces, brancbiostegals and anal rays many, 15 to 16, anal not striped *tschawylscha*. aa. Anal fin short, fewer than 12 developed rays, the last not much shorter than the first, the entire fin thus having a convex outline or margin, the height great in proportion to length of base Trout and Charr. b. Parr marks as bars, body compressed, depth carried well toward tail.. trout. bb. Parr marks as roundish blotches with mottling above and below, body less compressed, tapering rapidly toward tail Charr.

The Humpback Salmon, *Oncorhynchits gorbuscha* (Walbaum).

The humpback fry (pi. i, fig. 3) at the time of closure of the ventral walls average about 35 to 36 mm. in total length. Depth, greatest just behind pectorals, 6 in length (exclusive of caudal rays); in ill-nourished examples the slenderness becomes marked, this usually quite notable in late migrants; head about 3.5; eye 2.5 in head; nose round and blunt, tip of lower jaw scarcely reaching profile; contour in front of dorsal fin little arched; lunation of caudal slight; pectoral rounded, 2 or a little more in head (measured from axil to tip of longest ray); longest ray of dorsal about 2.5 to 3; longest ray of anal 3 to 3.75; greatest length of ventral equal to or somewhat greater than greatest height of anal;.gillrakers long and close-set, about 5-13 developed, longest equal to half diameter of pupil, and to the distance from first to fourth (3 interspaces) at upper end of lower limb.

In life, back green to bronzy, changing to indigo blue upon death; the sides silvery with brassy luster and green tints; ventral surface silvery white, usually without marks of any kind, but rarely with a few faint short parr marks above the lateral line; a narrow median dark line on back; membranes of caudal greenish, with black punctulations; dorsal similar with a narrow darker front margin; pectorals and lower fins colorless; iris greenish silver.

In preserved specimens, particularly formalin specimens, a magnifier shows minute punctulations over almost the entire side, the back, and the dorsal and caudal membranes, and sometimes on the maxillary, chin, and throat.

The humpback fingerling (pi. n, fig. 2) is little changed from the fry described, except in size. It is the most slender species of the genus, with head long and pointed. In 20 examples from Karluk Beach 65 to 92 mm. in total length, the average depth was 5.57 in length to base of middle caudal rays, extremes 5.12 to 6; in 6 examples 83 to 92 mm. long the depth was 5.54, head 4.4, eye 3.8 in head, pectoral a little less than 2, dorsal 2.26, anal a little more than 3, ventral 2.46. Branchiostegals 11-12 to 12-13; gillrakers 10 to 13 upper limb and 16 to 19 in lower limb, longest from 1J to 1J times diameter of pupil and spanning 4 to 5 interspaces. The length and number of the gillrakers is not infrequently greater than in the sockeye fingerling, but the absence of visible scales in the smaller individuals, and their delicacy and small size in the larger of the humpbacks, as well as the more slender body outline, will distinguish these fingerlings from the sockeye. In the adult humpback the gillrakers are 11-17 to 13-19, the longest 1J to 2 times diameter of pupil, covering 4 interspaces.

Colors of the fingerling: The dusky of the dorsal shows as a diffuse blotch on the front and distal portions, the dusky of caudal more intense toward the points of the lobes and at the base, but less marked than in the dog salmon; a little dusky appears in the axil of pectoral. A few small black blotches on the upper side were noted in a few of some fingerlings reared at the Clackamas station.

At this stage the scales, though very thin and delicate, may be made out with a magnifier or a good eye. The lateral line is a mere furrow and shows no tubing. In the dog salmon of the same or much less size the scales are evident and tubes of the lateral line distinct.

In the Karluk specimens examined the ovaries are ribbon-like, whereas in other species the ovaries are more cylindrical and usually somewhat swelled at the anterior end.

The Doo Salmon, *Oncorhynchus keta* (Walbaum).

The dog-salmon fry (pi. i, fig. 5) attains a length of about 40 mm. by the time the ventral walls are fully united, perhaps a greater length than the fry of any other salmon of the genus. It resembles the humpback in general shape. Greatest depth just behind pectorals, 5. 5 to 6 in body; head 4; eye about 2. 66 in head; pectoral 1.75 to 2; dorsal about 2; anal about 2.5; ventral equal to anal; gillrakers little more than tubercles, about 5-11 to 12 may be made out, longest about one-fourth diameter of pupil, equal to about one interspace.

In life, ground color bright grass green, becoming slightly darker on back and paling on lower side to an overcast on the silver; occasionally a brassy luster on back; lower parts silvery with the palest green iridescence; back with very fine black punctulations, fusing into numerous small black spots about the size of pupil from nape to base of caudal; a median dark line on back in front of dorsal, not marked back of dorsal. The punctulations cover sides to axil of pectoral in front, to about halfway between lateral line and ventrals, and surround caudal peduncle, becoming coarse and scattered below. The parr marks, from 6 to 12 in number, lie mainly above lateral line.

Pectoral and lower fins uncolored, caudal and dorsal greenish, fading distally, black punctulations on membranes, dorsal with blackish front margin. Iris brassy.

In preserved specimens the general color is silvery, with the dusky shades as described for the humpback, but never so dark on the back. Parr marks along lateral line elliptical or oval in shape, narrower and longer (deeper) toward the head; greatest diameter equal to eye, usually more numerous and narrower than in the sockeye, and not becoming bars as in the coho and king; also more subdued by the silver overcast than in the two last-mentioned species; along median dorsal line a row of small blotches sometimes coalescent into a mere stripe, the area between this and the parr marks usually spotted with round dots less than half diameter of pupil; occasionally a few broken blotches below. Dorsal and caudal membranes and first ray of pectoral dusky; other fins immaculate.

The dog-salmon fingerling (pi. n, fig. 3) is less slender in outline than the humpback, which, except that the dog salmon is obviously scaled, it otherwise resembles.

In 26 examples from Whidby Island, taken June 30, 1903, 78 to 122 mm. total length, sexes in equal numbers, the average depth is 5.1 in body (4.87-5.4); head 4.4; eye 3.3 in head; pectoral 2—; dorsal 2+; anal 3; ventral 2.4; developed anal rays 13 and 14; branchiostegals 13-13 to 14-15; gillrakers 8-12 to 9-15, longest about equal to pupil, spanning about 3 interspaces (sometimes only 2); scales 130 to 146, average 139. In specimens from Dundas Bay, July 24, 67 to 103 mm., the gillrakers are somewhat shorter, $ to once the diameter of pupil, covering 2 to 3J interspaces; scales 129 to 136, average 132.

In fingerlings from Naha Bay, July 2, 50 to 65 mm. in length, the parr marks are still apparent. In sea-run examples from Karluk Beach, July 24, up to 100 mm., they scarcely show through the scales, but are quite evident when the scales are stripped. The other coloration much as in the late fry stage; chin dusky; several rays of the pectoral with punctulations; tip of dorsal, except last ray, distinctly black; tip of caudal black, marked even in fork, this black tip of caudal distinguishing them roughly from the humpback of the same size, though the scaling must be the final test.

The Kino Salmon, *Onmrhynchus tschawytscha* (Walbaum).

The young king salmon (pi. I, fig. 4, figure and description from Karluk River specimens) at the time of the complete union of the ventral walls are from 35 to 37 mm. average length. In general outline they are less slender and tapering than the humpback or dog salmon. The depth, greatest in the region of front of dorsal, 4.25 in body; head about 3. 33 to 3.5; eye 2.5 in head; pectoral 1. 75, vertical fins high, dorsal 1.5; anal 2; ventrals 2.33; gillrakers about 4-11, short and well separated, longest equal to one-half diameter of pupil, spanning 1 interspace. The increased number of branchiostegal and anal fin rays (about 16 in each) help to distinguish this species.

Ground color of specimens in alcohol silvery, and except breast and in front of ventrals, with fine punctulations; about 9 to 12 long narrow parr marks usually equal to or greater in width than the silvery interspaces and lying about equally on either side of lateral line; a dark median dorsal line in front of dorsal fin, not so evident in caudal region; between this and the parr marks numerous round or oval blotches about size of pupil, the larger of these alternating with the parr marks so that it gives the upper end of these the appearance of being symmetrically margined by the silvery of the ground color; caudal lunation comparatively deep. In the Sacramento the caudal sometimes has a reddish tinge, and shades of yellow may appear on the ventrals and anal.

Yearlings (pi. m) from Karluk Lagoon, about 137 mm. long, have the following measurements: Depth 4.4; head 4; eye 3.5-4; pectoral 1.6-1.7; dorsal 1. 8-2; anal 2.3-3; ventral 2.2-2.3; greatest depth about midway between pectoral and dorsal, gracefully tapered to tip of the rather sharp nose. Gillrakers 10-13; longest equal to or less than diameter of pupil, spanning about 2 interspaces. (In adults 10731—07 2 from Oregon the longest gillraker is about 1$ to 2 times diameter of pupil, covering 3 interspaces.)

Color silvery, dark above; top of head, back, and sides to lateral line more or less thickly spotted with small roundish black spots about half diameter of pupil and less; distal portion of dorsal dusky, sometimes nearly black; caudal dusky; inner side of outer rays of pectoral dusky; anal and ventrals unmarked; parr marks visible under silver. Distinguished at sight from coho by the longer anal and the usually somewhat smaller eye, but definitely by the more numerous and finer branchiostegals and greater number of pyloric coeca.

The Coho Salmon, *Oncarhynchus kisutch* (Walbaum).

The coho fry (pi. i, fig. 6) at the time of hatching is about 27 mm. in total length, the sac about 10 mm. The greater size and the peculiar shape of the yolk sac distinguish the coho from the sockeye.

These fry average about 35 mm. total length at closure of ventral walls. The ventral membrane on either side of the ventral fins is persistent for a long period. In general shape the coho fry and small fingerlings much resemble the king salmon. Greatest depth just in front of dorsal, about 5 in body; thence diminishing toward nose; dorsal outline arched; head about 3.75; eye 2.5 in head; pectoral 2; vertical fins high, the front rays in both soon becoming extended; dorsal about 1.75; anal 2; ventrals 2.75; caudal lunation shallow. Gillrakers very short, little more than tubercles, about 5-10.

In Steelhead Creek, May 29, migrating fry had a ground color of smoky green with brassy iridescence, black punctulations everywhere except on throat and breast; these punctulations finest and most numerous on back, becoming coarser and more scattered on lower side; lower side with a red overshade or iridescence; membranes of fins with punctulations, but on pectoral and ventral these punctulations only close to body; remainder of these fins brownish orange; caudal-fin membranes orange ground, the fine black punctulations giving a dark effect, upper and lower (dorsal and ventral) margins clear brown, most pronounced on rudimentary rays, membrane between ray branches colored and dotted as between rays; membranes of dorsal with very pale orange shade deepening on rear, front with black margin equal in width to a central membrane, sometimes a narrow orange margin in front of this; anal membranes distinctly orange with punctulations as in caudal, these becoming close near margin at extremity of long rays and forming a black band about equal in width to two rays and joining membrane, tips of these rays and membranes white, giving the fin a white front margin and a black submargin equal to two or three times the width of white; adipose with orange front and top margin; dentary surface of mandible orange-brown at tip; maxillary uncolored, with scattered punctulations; iris bronzy to brassy; cheek with bronzy ground; opercular face dark; parr marks one-third to one-fourth as wide as long, increasing posteriorly in relative width (antero-posterior), and extending about equally above and below lateral line, the first partly under opercular flap, the last roundish and usually about under adipose fin, the penultimate sometimes under adipose; a narrow dark median line on back; smaller round spots on back sometimes alternate with parr marks. Viewed from above in water, the back shows ground color bronzy, with a few scattered dark spots, narrow supraorbital stripes ending at nostril, the median dark line showing distinctly with bronze bands of about equal width on either side.

In alcohol entire surface dusky, with punctulation except on a little of breast, some of the lower surface of head, and the paired fins. Parr marks present as 8 or 9 short and narrow bars, about one-half the width of the interspaces (variable but not usually so broad as in the king), and equal in length (depth) to about half depth of body, lying about evenly divided by lateral line, becoming more nearly round toward the caudal; a dark blotch at base and front of dorsal; tips of front anal rayB immaculate, forming a distal white stripe along front of fin.

A fingerling 58 mm. in length (pi. n, fig. 4) has a depth of 4 in body; head 3.5; eye 3 in head; pectoral 1.5; dorsal (longest ray) 1.33; anal 1.25; ventral 2 (some of the first dorsal and anal rays are variably produced); gillrakers, 8-14, longest one-half diameter of pupil, spanning about 2 interspaces.

Markings much as in earlier stages, but with additional markings on back. Short oval or triangular blotches appear between the parr marks, and numerous small, round, dark spots become irregularly scattered over entire upper surface, including top of head. The orange tints of the fry and smaller fingerlings largely disappear at about this size, the time of the change varying greatly in different localities. In the same'degree the falcation of anal and dorsal shows local and individual variation, but it is always notable. The tips of the first 4 to 6 rays of both these fins, with the outer membrane, retain the orange color or become white, to form a stripe about half the width of the pupil at the margin of the fin; this lies upon a submarginal band of black of similar width. The distinctness of these bands is variable, but in no case are they entirely absent in fingerlings of 40 to 100 mm., or even more, when in fresh water. At a certain point the elongated rays seem to stop growth in extension while the remainder of the fin continues its normal increase in size until the permanent form has been reached, after which all the growth proceeds together. Examples of 130 to 150 mm. show traces of the peculiarity of both growth and color, but later there is no variation from the normal shape as found also in the king.

A sea-run yearling (pi. iv) from Karluk Beach, June 18, 1903, 150 mm. in length, had depth 4.75; head 4; eye 3.66 in head; snout nearly equal to eye; pectoral 1.5; dorsal 2; anal 2.8; ventral 2; gillrakers 9-14, longest equal to diameter of pupil, spanning about 3 interspaces (in adults from 1§ to 2 times pupil, spanning 2 to 4 interspaces). Life colors (Itutter) "back olive brown, thickly spotted with black, dorsal dusky, except last ray is pale. Caudal yellowish by transmitted light, tip dusky, the dusky portions greater on lobes; pectoral yellowish; parr marks distinct; iris»somewhat golden." In alcohol 11 parr marks quite distinct, a little broader than interspaces and depth about half depth of body, spots on back round, the largest about J diameter of pupil, covering top of head and back as far as lateral line—extending on to upper edge of caudal; anal and pectorals with very few punctulations, lower parts silvery.

The Sockeye, *Oncorhynchus nerka* (Walbaum).

The sockeye fry at time of hatching measures some 24 mm. in total length, the sac itself about 9 mm., varying in individuals. The yolk sac is approximately cylindrical in general outline, sometimes slightly deeper (dorso-ventrally) at the posterior end. It has little tendency to become pointed at the posterior ventral extremity, as in the coho.

The ventral walls become completely united and the yolk disappears externally when the young sockeye measures about 32 mm. in total length. At this stage both dorsal and ventral outlines are arched (the dorsal the more in alcoholic specimens by reason of the contraction of the softer ventral tissues). The greatest depth is near the middle of the body just in front of the dorsal, about 4.75 to 5.5 in length to base of caudal rays (end of scaling). In poorly nourished examples the depth is greatly decreased in proportion to the length. Head about 3.75; nose rounded, blunt, length about equaling half diameter of eye; eye about 2.5 inhead; pectoral and dorsal about 2; anal and ventral about 2.66 in head; gillrakers 5-14, in length about two-fifths diameter of pupil, spanning 2 to 3 interspaces.

General color silvery, becoming dusky above. There is less tendency to metallic iridescence than in the coho, and the fins do not show the orange tints of the latter. The ventral surface is immaculate, including all the lower fins. The fine punctulations with which the upper parts are shaded extend from just behind the gill-openings to slightly below the lateral line and posteriorly approach more and more the ventral surface until, at the caudal peduncle, they reach the lower fin membrane. The individual punctulations are larger and more separated on the lower side; the close setting above gives the back a marked dusky color. The membranes of the rayed dorsal and the caudal are similarly dusky. A single row of small blotches sometimes merging together occupies the median dorsal line from top of head to base of caudal. Along the lateral line or a little below it anteriorly the parr marks appear, from seven to ten small, rounded, or elliptical blotches about half the diameter of the eye and more or less evenly distributed between the gill-openings and base of caudal; t he depth of color and the approach to circularity of outline increase toward the caudal region; a dark spot on the opercle and one at the base of caudal complete this row. A second row of similar but smaller blotches sometimes appears between the lateral row and the median dorsal line. In transparent specimens the black of the inner ventral linings may show through slightly. Tip of chin dusky.

The small fingerlings (pi. 1, fig. 2), 35 to 50 mm. in length, show some change in shape. The caudal peduncle becomes slim in proportion to the length and the general outline is more tapering; the greatest depth, at a point about midway between base of pectorals and front of dorsal, is about 5 in body; both ventral and dorsal outlines arc more nearly straight to base of caudal than in small fry. In larger and well-fed examples the ventral outline is slightly more arched. In poorly nourished and unthrifty examples the great est depth is through base Sockoye fingerl1ngs. Upper figure a..,,, Jt J tt ij i.i' poorly nour1shed example, lower of pectorals, the caudal peduncle looks deep and thin well nour1shed. in comparison, and the depth in front of dorsal is less than one-fifth the body length. (See text figures.)

In markings the general duskiness encroaches on the ventral region, only the belly, breast, and lower head parts (except the chin) remaining immaculate. The median dorsal marking may be a row of blotches, or these may merge into a nearly solid stripe, which in individuals of 50 mm. up usually fades into the general duskiness. In most of the smaller individuals the parr marks are rounded blotches little larger than the pupil, varying in number from 8 to 12 and more or less evenly distributed along the lateral line. The second row above may or may not be present.. Specimens from Karluk between 40 and 50 mm. long show considerable variation from the markings just described. The parr marks are elliptical, about twice as deep as wide, except over anal and on peduncle. These long bars are mainly *below* the lateral line. They much resemble the markings of the dog salmon. These specimens also vary from the more southerly examples in the smallness of the eye and in the fewer and shorter gillrakers. Their identification is not absolute.

At about 80 mm. length (pi. n, fig. 1) the fingerling assumes the graceful outlines of the adult, depth 4.5-5 in body, average 4.6; head 3.661.12, average about 4; eye nearly 3 in head, pectorals 1.5-2, average 1.66; dorsal 1.66-2.3, average 1.8; anal about 2.5; ventrals about 2; gillrakers very variable, 12-20 to 13-22; longest J to once diameter of eye, spanning 3 to 6 interspaces. In fresh water the general color is silvery over dark. Punctulations cover the entire body, except a narrow area between chin and ventrals. The parr marks are more or less elliptical, with a depth about equal to diameter of eye and almost obliterated by the silvery. Occasional freshwater specimens wholly silvery, sea-run individuals probably always so.

Ayearling(pl. v), from Karluk Beach, 165 mm. in length, had depth 5; head little more than depth, 4.5; eye about 3.5 in head; pectoral 1.5; dorsal 2.2; anal 2. 66; ventral 2; gillrakers as in adult—that is, having about the same proportion to diameter of pupil.. In life "back grassy green, thickly spotted; a dark blotch on distal half of anterior dorsal rays, posterior rays colorless; tips of caudal lobes dusky; lower lins colorless; no trace of parr marks; iris washed with golden" (Rutter). In alcohol the dark of the back reaches the lateral line in front, then lists under dorsal to about the fifth row of scales above lateral line, and on caudal peduncle approaches the line to about third row of scales. Numerous round dark spots about one-third diameter of pupil on back from nape to caudal, sometimes falling into about 2 irregular rows on each side, with others scattered, sometimes wholly irregular and often continuing on to top of head; the interspaces about twice size of spots. Dusky of dorsal includes all but tips of last 3 or 4 rays; axil and inner surface of upper part of pectoral slightly dusky; tip of chin and adipose fin dusky. When scales are removed, round parr marks may be noted in specimens up to 200 mm. in length.

Almost from the first free-swimming stage the sockeye may be distinguished from any species except the humpback by the length, number, and fineness of the gillrakere. The humpback at times exhibits a greater number of gillrakers, and these of greater proportionate length, than the sockeye from the same locality. In this case, however, the small sockeye fingerlings may be recognized by the color, and the larger by their coarser scales, greater depth, and larger eye.

The Steelhead Trout, *Salmo gairdneri* (Richardson).

There are three accepted species of trout in Alaskan waters—the steelhead, rainbow, and cutthroat. I have been able to find but one type of fry, and am even unable to find distinguishing marks in the young of known species grown in the hatcheries. The fry here described 1 have called steelhead, for the reason that it is found in abundance migrating to the sea from streams in which large numbers of steelheads are known to spawn. The description may be taken in general as applying also to the rainbow and cutthroat trout fry.

This fry (pi. i, fig. 7), at the time of closure of the ventral walls, averages between 30 and 32 mm. in total length. Depth about 6; head 3.5 in body; eye 3 in head; pectoral 1.66; dorsal 2; anal-2. 25; ventral 2.5. Head pointed; greatest depth through middle in front of dorsal;

gillrakers very short and well separated; about 5-10 to be made out by counting the faintly developed tubercles, longest about one-third diameter of pupil, equal to or less than one interspace.

General color silvery, sometimes with brassy iridescence, parr marks 9 to 12, deep and narrow, usually dark and contrasting sharply with the silvery interspaces. Body, except belly in front of ventrals, and fins, except the paired ones, with punctulations; dorsal with front rays black; anal with posterior rays less shortened than in salmon, which character with the fewer rays gives the fin a more rounded appearance

The Charr, Or Dolly "varden Trout, *Salvelinus nalma* (Walbaum).

The charr fry (pi. i, fig. 8) has undergone complete absorption of _ the yolk sac at 26 mm. length. It is slender, with greatest depth through pectoral, much resembling in shape and general appearance the larger sockeye of a somewhat later stage. Depth about 5 in body; head 3.5; eye 3 in head; pectoral 1.5; dorsal 1.66; anal 2.25; ventral 2.5; gillrakers about 4 to 7 or 8, somewhat longer in proportion than in the steelhead, longest equal to about one-half eye, equal to or slightly greater than an interspace.

Of lighter general ground color than the steelhead, the parr marks occurring as 7 to 10 round blotches about the size of the eye, along lateral line; other similar blotches on back. Lower fins immaculate. Readily distinguishable by the slim tapering shape, general brownish color, size and shape of blotches, and anal fin.

In fingerlings, about 40 mm. long, depth about 4.5, greatest between dorsal and pectoral; head 3.66; eye nearly 4 in head; pectoral 1.4, dorsal 1.6; anal and ventral about 1.87; gillrakers about 5-9, the longest about equal to diameter of the very small pupil and spanning one interspace. An irregular row of alternating blotches below the parr marks, faintly present in fry, becomes more distinct and the back becomes thickly mottled with spots about size of pupil; otherwise the color much as in fry. This species is unusually thick (laterally) in proportion to depth, and is not so much flattened as the salmons and true trouts. This character becomes noticeable in the fingerlings, and together with the peculiar mottling makes them readily distinguishable without counting the anal.

THE BASINS STUDIED.

The two regions from which most of the original material in this paper is derived are the basins of the Naha and the Karluk rivers. From the Naha as a central locality, the conditions existing in adjacent basins received some attention, and salmon from Yes Bay, Karta Bay, Moira Sound, Boca de Quadra, and the streams of Annette Island were examined. These latter waters have been described in the reports of the operations of the steamer *Albatross* in Alaska." The accompanying sketch map of the Naha region illustrates typical conditions as found in most of the smaller sockeye streams in Alaska.

CONDITIONS CONTROLLING THE WORK.

The Naha as an observation station is ill adapted for a small party on account of its complexity and extent, though rendered advantageous by the Alaska Packers' Association establishment and the generous assistance extended by that corporation. The successful conduct of any inquiry, however, requires either a sufficient number of observers to carry on the work simultaneously at all parts of the area to be covered, or a sufficiently small area to permit the party available to cover the entire territory readily; and of indispensable importance in fishery investigations is sufficient apparatus, such as boats, suitable nets, etc., to apply continuously any given line of experiment or study. For the best work on the Naha the absolute control of at least 4 boats would have been necessary, and even with this complement, the distance from the nearest habitable quarters at the mouth of the stream to the spawning ground of the fish is such that the round trip is practically a day's journey, leaving little time for observations en route or at the extremity of the trip. Another complicating feature, objectionable from one standpoint, desirable from another, is the presence of the brackish-water lagoon. Had it been possible readily to reach the mouth of the river above the lagoon, the trap could have been set there, as was to be desired; the lagoon , » Moser, Bulletin U. S. Fish Commission, vol. xvm, 1898, p. 1-178, and vol. xxi, 1901, p. 173-398, and 39901. It should be noted that in the descriptions of the Moira Sound region, vol. xvm, p. 78-80, the descriptions for Kegan and Old Johnson stream have been transposed; the figures for the catch, however, are correctly assigned.

would thus have been a part of the saltwater approaches. Under the circumstances, however, it was necessary to operate the trap at the rapids below the lagoon, where it was subject to the rise and fall of tide. This necessity may to a certain extent have altered results.

METHOD USED TO DETERMINE MIGRATORY MOVEMENTS.

The apparatus used for taking the migrating young was a sort of fyke trap made from a regulation collecting seine used by the Bureau, and was similar in principle of operation to the gear used by Rutter in the California investigation and by Babcock in the Fraser (p. 30). The conversion of the seine into a trap was accomplished by sewing on a bag of coarse bobbinet to surround and extend beyond the netting bag of the seine. This latter was then opened and a small funnel of bobbinet laced to the opening. The large bobbinet bag was closed at the hinder end by tying with a cord, so that it could be readily opened and the contents shaken into a bucket. With a short seine pole and bridle at either end the contrivance was then ready to hang across the current for operation. For successful results the current must be sufficiently rapid to keep the bag distended—otherwise the fish will not enter it—yet not strong enough to burst the fabric. In water too swift the smaller fish are pressed against the web and drowned. The rise and fall of the tide at station 2 in the Naha vitiated the statistics to a degree. With such a contrivance careful weight must be given to the state of the water. Muddy, swift water as at flood time always shows an increased catch, due doubtless in part to the favorable influence on the operation of the apparatus as well as to increased movement of the fish.

This apparatus as ordinarily operated is very defective. Estimates of numbers of migrating fish based upon its results can be only very distantly approximate. In no case can the entire current of a large stream be occupied, and only in exceptional cases will the net at all times reach from top to bottom. In the Naha and Sacramento tests, the lead line was frequently some distance from the bottom; in the Fraser River inquiry, however, it appears that the net was set on the bottom. Only by repeated tests can it be determined on which side of the stream the net will be most effective. On the Sacramento I made a few tests as to its efficacy at the side and center of the channel, respectively, but results were not definite, since other factors necessarily entered into the question. A complete experiment would require several of these traps to be operated simultaneously in different parts of the stream. In any current where fine-meshed fabric can hold, moreover, the stronger fish can breast the stream and escape. This defect of the device used is called to attention by Mr. Babcock in his report for British Columbia. The objections stand only against estimates of total number of migrants based on the catch made.

THE NAHA. CHARACTER OF THE STREAM.

The Nana River rises in the upper central part of Revillagigedo Island, Southeast Alaska. Its extreme upper part has not been explored, but doubtless possesses no characters of note differing from the usual mountain stream of that region. As a whole the stream is somewhat peculiar in the large number of lakes (four) in its course, but the total surface area of these four lakes is no greater in proportion to the volume of the stream than may be found in other instances, for example, the Karta River. The upper two of these lakes are of no great importance to the present salmon run, since a fall of some 30 feet, together with a series of broken cascades below the ower one, now prevents the ascent of the salmon. The two lakes are connected by a short reach of the stream which offers no obstruction to the passage of fish between them. The lower one, known as Patching Lake, is well stocked with cutthroat and Dolly Varden trout, and seems to contain also the dwarf form of the sockeye. In the spring of 1903 a plant of sockeye fry' was made in the connecting stream, making the original presence of the dwarf form subject to some doubt. Patching Lake is the largest of the four lakes and is probably the deepest. It is between 2 and 3 miles in length and less than one-half mile in width. Depths of 140 feet have been sounded.

In the lower course of the river, and yet accessible to salmon, are two lakes, Heckman Lake, about 1$ miles in length, and Jordan Lake, of about 1 mile. At the mouth of the stream is a brackish-water lagoon, about 1 mile in length, known as Roosevelt Lagoon. This latter receives the salt water from Naha Bay at ordinary and spring tides. Its surface water shows brackish everywhere except in time of flood waters, and the greater depths are doubtless quite salt.

The greatest depth in Heckman Lake is about 130 feet, in Jordan Lake somewhat less. The area and shallowness of these lakes, together with their exposed situation, admit of an early acquisition of high surface temperatures. Fortmann Hatchery is located at the head of Heckman Lake adjacent to the most important natural spawning ground of the sockeye. These beds are about 6 miles from tide water, one-half of this distance being occupied by the lagoon and lakes. As originally found they were about 400 yards in length and of perhaps 15 or 20 yards average width, the whole more or less covered with logs and drift. In addition to these, small parts of the section of the river connecting Jordan and Heckman lakes were used; also McCune Creek at the upper end of Heckman Lake, and unimportant areas of Emma Creek, a small tributary of Jordan Lake. All of these beds are also frequented by the coho and humpback salmon, but the greater number of these two species do not reach Heckman Lake. Their most prolific grounds are that section of the main river between the lagoon and Jordan Lake, a large area being afforded by the stream just below and immediately above Dorr Falls. In addition they occupy the many small creeks which enter the lagoon, the river, and the lakes. King and dog salmon enter the Naha in too small numbers to indicate their preferences, but king salmon have been seined at the hatchery, and it is probable that in all such streams they go as far upstream as possible. But one king salmon fry was taken during the present work, that from the lower river on June 11, 1903. A few dog-salmon fry were noted migrating from Gibson Creek. They formed a scarcely notable percentage in the catches in the main stream.

A considerable part of the shores of both Heckman and Jordan lakes is of gravel and apparently not unsuitable for "nests." It may be that when the stream was crowded the shores were used, but at no time were sockeyes observed to spawn about the lake shores' as in other basins. The portion of the stream between these two lakes was not inspected, but the area of suitable ground for beds is said to be small, the channel being very rough. A few cohos spawn just above Jordan Lake, but inspection by the hatchery superintendent has shown that the sockeyes do not frequent this section of the river.

YIELD OF SALMON.

As a sockeye stream the Naha has been one of the most productive of the smaller streams of Southeast Alaska, a fact which may be due in part to its having been so unremittingly fished. The long, narrow bay which receives the river furnished excellent fishing grounds, and the shallow upper end an excellent foundation for a fence. In the following table is shown in round numbers the yield of the Naha and the important adjacent streams for each year from 1887 to 1900:

The Catch Of Sockeyes From The Naha River, In Thousands.

The large catch in 1891 was due to close fencing as well as abundance of fish. It will be noted, as shown in the accompanying block table, that the decline in numbers, while in general gradual, is most marked in four-year periods after this date. It also will be remarked that the heavy catches do not coincide in the different basins, pointing to a shifting of the general run under different circumstances. Conclusions based on the commercial catches, however, require not only accuracy in the statistics, but details as to the efforts made to take all fish arriving in the given waters. These details, unfortunately, we do not have. Yet these figures undoubtedly indicate the possibility of fishing out a given stream, and with this is carried the implication that at least the greater part of the supply of any stream must be derived from the fry produced in that stream.

CATCH OF YOUNG SALMON IN THE TRAP. To determine facts regarding the migration of the young salmon into salt water, a trap such as is described on page 21 was placed below Hirsch Rapids on the Naha, at station 2 (see map, p. 112). The location was chosen on account of its accessibility, as stated above. The catch made by this apparatus is shown in the following table (no. 1). As the trap was operated in salt water, the catches included sticklebacks, perch, blennies, occasional trout, etc., which are grouped under "Other fishes."

Table 1.—Catch Made By Trap At Station 2, Naha Bay, 1903 And 1904.

During the season of 1903 a 35-foot trap was used except where otherwise indicated in the table; in 1904 a 45-foot trap.

In 1903, in 17 sets of the trap at Hirsch Rapids, station 2, between April '21 and August 12, on only three occasions were sockeye fry taken, twice a single example and the other time fifteen. In six trials from April 21 to May 11 no sockeyes were taken; on May 17, 23, 24, and June 2, a total of over 2,000 sockeye yearlings from 52 to 97 mm. total length, together with over 2,500 humpback fry, were taken. Thus it would seem if any great number of sockeye fry were migrating more would have been found in the net.

In 1904, between May 17 and June 30, at the same point, over 8,300 sockeye yearlings were taken, as well as over 3,300 humpback fry and nearly 350 coho fry, but no sockeye fry.

In 1903 a trap was placed in the Naha at station 1 as soon as the lagoon was sufficiently clear of ice to permit use of a boat, April 12 to 19, thus probably securing the earliest movement of humpback fry. At this time all the lakes above were entirely covered with ice. April 19 a set at station 3, just below Jordan Lake, took only humpback and dog-salmon fry. It can not be that the run of sockeye fry was over before the work was begun, since great numbers were only recently hatched, nor is it likely that it occurs later in the summer, for no fry of any kind were taken in a trap set August 12, 1903, July 9, 10, and September 2, 1904, nor in one set in the outlet of Yes Lake, July 18 to 21, and August 5 to 26, 1905.

A remote opportunity for error lies in the fact that, Roosevelt Lagoon being salt water at the bottom, a deep-water fish, which the young sockeye undoubtedly is to an extent, might pass the rapids at high water and go under the trap. But this is extremely improbable, since in British Columbia waters, where the migration has been studied, the fry passed in the same manner and at the same season as the yearlings. It is further shown to be unlikely by the fact that a trap set below the mouth of Jordan Lake at station 3, May 15,16, and 17, 1903, took only 2 or 3 sockeye fry, while securing some 12,000 humpback. At the same point June 2 and 3 only 14 sockeye fry were taken. At this date the humpback run was practically over. Nor did a trap set at the foot of Heckman Lake, station 4, May 12 to 14, show any considerable movement, 6 sockeye fry being taken, with 250 yearlings.

In 1903 the first movement of sockeyes at salt water was noted May 17. May 11 a trap set at station 2, in which over 1,000 humpback fry were taken, failed to secure any sockeyes. The migration probably began on the high water of May 12 to 15; 300 yearlings were taken on the latter date below Jordan Lake. May 17, 220 were taken in a trap spanning about one-third of the channel at station 2; on the 23d over 800 were secured by a trap of half the size, spanning about one-fifth the channel; in this small trap 375 were taken on the 24th and 650 on June 2. After this latter date the catch fell away; June 3, only 9 yearlings were taken below Jordan Lake, and at station 2 on the 13th and 14th but 5 were obtained.

These trials indicate that the migration in 1903 began about the middle of May and practically ended early in June, though stragglers continued to show into July. The maximum occurred about May 23, after high water in the river and on high tides in the bay.

In 1904 the run had begun before the work was commenced. The first trial was made at station 2, May 17, and though the trap was badly damaged, 10 yearlings were taken. On the 19th, with a trap covering about 60 per cent of the channel, 863 yearlings were secured. The run continued with variations till June 5, when a maximum catch of 1,157 was made. After this date the catch rapidly decreased, only 83 being taken on the 10th, 50 on the 13th, 4 on the 30th, and none July 9 and 10.

In comparing the runs of these two seasons it must be noted that the conditions varied materially. In 1903 the heavy ice kept the river closed until an unusually late date. The lakes were not entirely clear from ice until about May 12, and the temperature of the river did not rise above 40 until after the middle of May. In 1904, at the time of arrival of the working party, May 16, the river had reached a temperature of about 44 and the ice had been gone for several weeks. By the latter part of May the temperature had risen to 50, and by June 2 to 52. In 1903 this latter temperature was not reached till June 13, yet in 1904 the run continued over almost the same period as in 1903, reaching its maximum perhaps somewhat later. This fact must be related to the much greater output of the hatchery for the latter year. In 1902 about 10,000,000 fry were liberated, under primitive conditions; the following yeaf nearly 30,000,000 were planted under somewhat better conditions. The product of natural spawning is a negligible factor.

YES BAY STREAM.

Yes Bay is about 30 miles north of the Naha on Behm Canal. The river is somewhat larger than the Naha and about 1 mile in length below the lake. Yes Lake is nearly 4 miles in length and of average width less than one-half mile. The greatest depth is 230 feet. Above this lake the. river offers about three-fourths of a mile of excellent spawning ground, at the end of which the further ascent of fish is cut off by high falls. These falls were passable at one time, perhaps, as Dolly Varden trout have been taken above them. At a considerable elevation are other lakes of less extent that have not yet been explored.

Yes Lake has no tributaries that are occupied by spawners except the main stream. The sockeyes use the upper river above the lake. This section is also frequented by cohos, steelheads, and an occasional king. Humpbacks spawn mainly in the lower river. The Yes Bay hatchery is located on the section of the river immediately above the lake.

The trap maintained at the foot of Yes Lake July 18 to 21 and August 5 to 26, 1905, made no catch of migrating fry or yearlings. It was evident that the migration was entirely over at that time. A trap of the same kind installed during the spring of 1907 at the same point made heavy catches of young, but at the time of writing this report the material has not been specifically identified. Most of the data regarding the summer residence of young in the lake were drawn from observations in this locality.

KARLUK RIVER. SUITABILITY AS A SPAWNING STREAM.

The Karluk River is a much larger stream than the Naha. It is about 20 miles in length and several times the volume of the Naha. The lower course is one continual rapid, but presents no falls to obstruct the ascent of the fish. The upper course is of moderate current and affords excellent spawning ground, while in addition there arc many sloughs to act as nursery ponds for the young. The lake is estimated to be 8 miles in length and 2 in width, depth unknown; two much smaller lakes are tributary to the main body. There are numerous small streams entering the main lake, some of which, as the outlets of the tributary lakes, are of considerable length and suitable for spawning ground, while others are swift mountain torrents with rough beds which offer but small areas for the fish. The shores of the lakes also are utilized for spawning. The river proper falls into a lagoon some 2 miles in length, into which the salt water flows from about half tide, so that it is largely brackish. The outlet of this lagoon to the sea is narrow and gives rise to strong currents in each direction somewhat as in the Naha. Near the head of the lagoon is located the Karluk hatchery. The Karluk River has been good for an annual output of about 2,000,000 soekeyes, besides small runs of king and coho and occasional large runs of humpbacks.

MOVEMENTS OF YOUNG SALMON AS SHOWN BY TRIAL CATCHES.

The least inconvenient means of access to Karluk Lake is by portage from Larsens Cove, Uyak Bay, to Nicolai's barabara, a trip of 5 miles; thence by river, too shallow for a boat and too deep for good walking, 6 miles more to the lake. The labor required to bring to the lake the necessaries of life, and the consequent lack of scientific.

"A full description, by Dr. Tarlotnn H. Bean, may be found in Bulletin U. S. Fish Commission, vol. ix, 1889, p. 165 et seq.

outfit, will account for the meager results the observers obtained in certain lines.

At this station the main attention was given to adult fishes. These were taken in a small pound or trap spanning about one-fourth the outlet on the shoal side and built for taking the incoming fish. A trap for young was operated a few times in connection with this pound and was also set a few times in tributary creeks. The party was equipped with a single net so constructed, and the debris from the lake soon accomplished its ruin. On account of this shortage of proper gear the movement of fry and yearlings from Karluk Lake was not followed with any definiteness. Five sets were made with a 25-foot net rigged as above described, with the following results:

June 5, over night, sculpins, sticklebacks, 150 salmon parrs, a few salmon fry, a few trout fry.

June 25, over night (between pound and shore), 738 sculpins, 530 sticklebacks, 23 trout, 32 salmon parrs, 16 salmon fry.

June 27, over night, sculpins, sticklebacks, 8 trout, 2 salmon parrs, 2 salmon fry; 12 m. to 5 p. m., a few sculpins and sticklebacks.

June 28, over night, sculpins, sticklebacks, 1 salmon parr, no fry.

June 30, 12 m. to 4.30 p. m., 3 sculpins, 165 sticklebacks, 1 salmon parr.

It will be noted that all these results show but a slight movement of sockeye fry from the lake. It may be they had reached the river prior to the first set of the net, though not all had passed down the stream. Throughout May and June the sloughs of the upper part of the Karluk River contained many sockeye fry or small fingerlings. In a haul May 22 nearly a thousand were taken, many with remnants of yolk. June 21 large schools of small fingerlings were numerous in the upper river, and some were taken with the dip net. June 30 a few fingerlings averaging nearly 2 inches in length were taken in a pool of the river. Such fish seem to have disappeared soon after this date, since the observers made no further note of them. Fry and small fingerlings were abundant in the lagoon during June, July, and into August, but as these may have been the hatchery output, their presence indicates nothing regarding migration habits, except that they all apparently passed out into the sea during the summer.

It would seem that the. station party would have noted any large movement from the lake had it occurred, since their camp was established at its mouth early in May, before the ice had left it. But this is not necessarily true. At that season daylight lasts from about 3 a. m. till 10 p. m. The young salmon travel little in daylight, and it might easily be that a considerable movement could have occurred without remark. It might be thought possible that the numerous fry in the river were the product of eggs spawned below the lake by fish arriving after low temperatures obtained. That this is highly improbable, however, appears from the fact that such eggs could not have hatched and the young developed by the time the fry were noted. Ripe fish would scarcely fail to enter the lake up to the time that ice formed upon it. It was shown that while ice is on the lake the temperature of the river is not much above 34 F. At this temperature the sockeye eggs would require about two years to develop into migrating fry.

CONDITIONS REPORTED IN BRITISH COLUMBIA.

The observations made in British Columbia, under the direction of J. P. Babcock, on the Fraser and Wannuck rivers (see Annual Reports of the Fisheries Commissioner for British Columbia, 19021904) should be noted here. In the spring of 1902, following the big run of 1901, fry were abundant in Lake Creek, the outlet of Seton Lake, and apparently migrated downstream at the same time with the yearlings. In 1903 swimming fry were seen in Lake Creek as early as January, remaining till April. They seemed to move downstream in April and May, after which none was seen either in Lake Creek or in Seton Lake. The movement of the yearlings began on the spring floods early in April and continued to June, being the heaviest the first two weeks in May. Observations at Lytton, in the main river, found fry and yearlings, the latter least in number, traveling together between April 1 and July 13 in both the Fraser and Thompson rivers. In 1904 no fry or yearlings were found in the rivers. This was supposed to be due to the absence of spawners in the waters above in 1902 and 1903. It would seem, however, that if the movement of fry in 1903 was marked there should have been a corresponding number of yearlings to show in 1904. It is impossible to believe that the product of the 1902 eggs all left the waters as fry. Trials in the Wannuck River at Rivers Inlet, north of the Fraser, in 1904, discovered an abundant movement of both fry and yearlings between April 13 and July 1. The fry were in greater abundance than the yearlings and the height of the run was between May 22 and June 16. This greater abundance of fry as compared with the number of yearlings is thought by Mr. Babcock to be due merely to the operation of the trap. Both fry and yearlings drift downstream tail first. The tail coming in contact with the net, the fish would attempt to rush upstream and avoid the obstacle. If the net were set in water of moderate current the stronger yearlings would be able thus to avoid it and escape, whereas the weaker fry would be more likely to enter it. In swift currents both are forced into the trap.

SUMMARY OF OBSERVATIONS.

From these various records it would seem that in the larger rivers, as the Karluk and Fraser, many sockeye fry leave their nursery waters as soon as they are able to swim and feed, or at the beginning of the fingerling stage; that in the smaller streams, as the Naha, this number is small and, in comparison to the number resident for one season, negligible; that in all cases a portion, perhaps the greater, remain in the lakes for one winter and migrate in the following spring as yearlings. Whether any spend a second winter in the fresh water has not been demonstrated. This residence of large numbers of young in fresh waters with a definite and apparently anticipated movement seaward the second spring of their existence is unique in this species. While some king and coho young spend the summer in the vicinity of their birthplace there is no evidence that these summer residents do not pass to the sea as a rule during the fall, or for that matter at any convenient time. Their continued stay seems to depend largely on the period of rainless weather that obtains on the Pacific coast during the summer months. Only a small remnant of the lake-inhabiting fingerlings of these two species spend a winter in fresh water. Humpback and dog salmon all leave for the sea almost as soon as they are able to swim. This habit of the sockeye is doubtless connected closely with the habit of lake spawning, or is even the immediate effect of that cause. Further, it probably has given rise to the dwarf form, of which no analogue exists in the other speciec.

YOUNG SALMON IN FRESH WATER.
THE SOCKEYE.
MOVEMENT OF FRY ABOVE THE LAKES.

The sockeye fry when hatched or planted in the tributaries of a lake linger a little while on the nursery ground. Small plants made in pools near Loring in 1903 remained a considerable time after the absorption of the yolk sac, and the same fact was noted at the nursery pond at Fortmann Hatchery the following year. Similar observations were made also at Karluk. The first creek entering at the foot of Karluk Lake is a small creek consisting of three pools connected by short rapids and fed entirely by springs. A few sockeyes frequent it for spawning, the greater percentage, apparently, being weak fish that are unable to continue'the journey. It may be, too, that this creek remains open late in the fall and finds favor with late-coming fish. On July 14 a net was set across the mouth, taking in daylight 4 adult salmon, 1 stickleback, and 1 sculpin. At night 6 adults and 87 young sockeyes, 7 sticklebacks and 1 sculpin were taken. Of these young 11 were feeding and had reached an average length of 41 mm. 10731—07 3

They contained insects, larva?, and crustaceans. The remainder were recently out of the fry stage, and only a few had begun to eat. This indicates that some of the young remained some time longer in the pools than they would have done in a stream of different character. Their late development is doubtless due to the cold spring water. Nets set across one of the principal spawning creeks on July 16 and 27 took very few fry.

After some days, perhaps when growing necessity for food demands activity, sockeye young, as fry or small fingerlings, drop down the stream into the lake or maybe the sea. During the season of observation on the Naha none was ever seen in the stream below the lakes, though cohos in abundance were resident there throughout the summer. Nbr were any ever seen by the writer about the margins of any Alaskan lakes except in the one instance mentioned below. Sockeyes apparently are never resident in the streams and never found in them except during the migratory movement.

While adequate observations are lacking, it is probable that the fry travel in schools. In the Karluk they were observed by Rutter to school while in the sloughs, though they have nowhere been seen to migrate in schools. In the lakes they remain during daylight in comparatively deep water. Rutter notes that they were at no time seen in abundance about the shores of Karluk Lake; Babcock states that they were not seen in Seton Lake after May. In the Naha lakes they were seen but once, June 11, a small school in Heckman Lake near the outlet, and a few in Jordan Lake in company with numerous cohos. They were taken in Alturas Lake outlet by Evermann on July 20 with fingerlings of the same species. Later in the season young sockeyes were obtained in Alturas Lake only by sinking the seine to the bottom in water of considerable depth, 15 to 60 feet. In Yes Lake in 1905 they were taken *by* surface hauls of a 130-foot seine after dark in the latter part of August and September, and the same means were used successfully in the Naha lakes later in that season.

FOOD AND FEEDING.

In the lakes and in all waters where such food is available, young sockeyes subsist largely upon small crustacea and associated forms, most of which have a diurnal movement to and from the surface, varying with the light. In the evening they rise to near the surface, and, with the coming of daylight, or shortly preceding day, retire to greater depths." In 1905 from August to November a number of tows with fine nets in Yes Lake and the Naha lakes showed that crustaceans are ordinarily absent from the surface during daylight. "The diurnal movement of plankton Crustacea, by Chaneey Juday. Transactions Wisconsin Academy *ot* Sciences, vol. xiv, 1904, p. 534-568.

They could be taken in small numbers by sinking the net several fathoms. In Klawak Lake, however, on October 1 copepods seem to have been abundant near the surface at any time of day, but this was noted in comparatively shallow water, whereas the trials on the other lakes had been made in water of greater depth. As these forms have little horizontal movement it may be that their-presence in Klawak Lake during the day was to be accounted for by the shallowness of the water.

On the approach of darkness many of these crustaceans congregate near the surface, and with that come the young sockeyes. Taken soon after dark, these young fish commonly had the stomach filled with crustacea, with a number of insects, mostly flies and winged ants, in the esophagus. Over the entire surface of Yes Lake on a quiet evening of August or September the presence of young fish could be marked by the ripples. Sometimes they would jump clear of the water, but more usually merely rise to the surface, apparently to snap.up the floating insects which they then sought. The depth at which the fish remain during daylight is unknown, but is probably not great. As noted above, they were obtained in Alturas Lake in 15 to 60 feet. Whether any lived at the greater depth is unknown, since the seine had to be landed through lesser depths. It is unlikely they much exceed such depth, since in summer the lower parts of small lakes are unsuitable for the support of animal life."

Small fingerlings taken in Karluk River May 22 were feeding on crustacea, insects, and insect larvae. June 21 their food was almost wholly insects and larvse; in the lagoon July 24 it was mainly insects, but with some crustacea. Specimens of slightly advanced size (average 42 mm.) from Wood River, Western Alaska, submitted by the collector without notes, contain both crustacea and insects. Some small fingerlings taken July 14 in the small creek tributary to Karluk Lake contained insects and in one instance crustacea.

In Yes Lake October 12 tows immediately off the mouth of the inflowing river in water of 47 F. took very few crustacea. These were probably not from the river water, for it, being somewhat colder, would sink to the greater depths on entering the lake. October 17 a net set over night in the river just above the lake took very few crustacea; river temperature 43 and lake 46 F. September 12 a net was set at the foot of the lake in the outflow for fifty minutes and no crustacea taken; at the same time tows were made just above this set net and a few crustacea taken, but much fewer than were usually taken in the main body of the lake. It would seem from these few trials that there is a scarcity of crustacea in both sections of the river, o See E. A. Birge, Gases dissolved in the waters of Wisconsin lakes. Transactions American Fisheries Society, 1906, p. 143-163.

but the matter needs further investigation. Even these slow-moving forms may be able to avoid the action of the current at the foot of lakes and remain within the lake boundaries. FOOD SUPPLY IN RELATION TO THE HATCHING SEASON.

The relation of food supply to the season of hatching has not yet been worked out. In the latitudes in which the sockeye is found it is improbable that any fry reach the feeding stage in advance of the opening of the streams from ice, unless when the spawn is deposited on the lake shores. In this latter event they would seek subsistence in the lake waters. It is shown above that these fingerlings feed to some extent upon surface forms when in streams or lakes at a season when such food is present. Their more natural food appears to be the subsurface plankton. The abundance of this material may be an important factor in determining the time of departure from fresh.water.

This question has an important bearing in fish cultural work. The use of spring or heated water may shorten the incubation period to such an extent that fry reach the feeding stage in advance of the natural production of their food. To liberate them in that event must be disastrous; to retain and feed them artificially nullifies the economic advantage obtained in hastening the incubation.

The temperature at which the most thrifty fry may be produced is another question that should be taken up. There are some data to show that low temperatures increase the number of temperature units required to effect the hatching. In long periods of depressed temperatures errors in the thermometer or its reading will be a greater factor than in short periods of observation. But if very cold water does retard the hatching, then such temperatures may or may not be advantageous. The success of certain methods in handling an insect-feeding species in waters that never freeze can be no criterion as to the best methods for a species of different habits living in different waters.

GROWTH IX FRESH WATER.
Fifty-nine young sockeyes taken in Yes Lake August 24, 1905, varied from about 32 to 66 mm. total length, with an average of about 46 mm.; 66 seined on September 10 varied from 35 to 75, with an average of 50 mm.; 59 taken September 26 and 27 varied between 34 and 82 mm., with an average of 45 mm. Assuming that these by the following spring would reach the same size as the Naha fish taken in 1903 when under the most nearly natural conditions, an average length of 65 mm., they would have to increase from 15 to 20 mm. in length from September to May.

Since the deeper water of the lakes will not fall much below 39 F., the point of maximum density, and since with the approach of cold weather the diffusion of oxygen will become more general, there seems to be no reason, unless there is a cessation of activity due to the cold, why fingerlings should not feed more or less during the winter. Some species of crustaceans are known to reach, their maximum numbers during the winter. This question has not been investigated for Alaskan lakes, nor are any data yet available upon which to base conclusions. Fry from the previous season's spawn in Yes Lake are ordinarily able to begin to feed about the middle of April, at which time they are somewhat over 30 mm. average length. By the latter part of August they have reached an average length of about 45 mm., a 50 per cent increase in a period of about four months. That this is crudely approximate is shown by averages in the three catches cited above.

Should the figures for the Naha yearlings show the approximate size of the Yes Lake migrants, these have little greater growth to make between August and May than they make between April and September. This would require little increase in size during the winter, since the lakes seldom freeze over before January, and up to that time feeding on the lake plankton can be continuous. Dr. Evermann's data from Alturas Lake, as showing rapidity of growth, are rendered inaccurate by the necessity of comparing small fingerlings from shallow water with the larger fish from deeper water, but show clearly that the yearlings there attain a larger size than in the Alaskan lakes studied. His specimens of July averaged 48 mm.; those of September 9, 83 mm.

It is interesting to note that while the young taken in Yes Lake in September did not fall below 45 mm., 46 specimens obtained in Heckman Lake October 2 averaged only 36 mm. and 28 taken on October 7 averaged but 40 mm. With this diminished size was noted a corresponding slimness and lean condition (fig., p. 18). It is also to be stated that the surface tows for food material in Heckman Lake, as compared with the material from Patching and Yes lakes, showed a diminution in number and general size of the crustacean life. These facts raise the question of the possibility of overstocking waters with fry. Of course, in case the surplus of young fish leave the parent waters as fry, as would seem to be indicated by the observations of the British Columbia parties, there could scarcely be any danger from this source. But the writer's observations in the Naha failed to reveal any such movement there and it is not unreasonable to suppose that some condition exists there which alters the habits of the fish in that respect. If that is true, and all the sockeye young spend one winter in the lake, then, with the increased millions which artificial hatching is able to turn out, a serious menace is offered to the natural food supply of the waters, since no steps are taken, or perhaps can be taken, to increase that supply. It is notable that Patching Lake, where wholly natural conditions yet exist, showed a more favorable supply of plankton life than Heckman Lake. In this connection it must also be noted that yearlings leaving the Naha in 1903 averaged about 65 mm. in length. In the following year there appeared a considerable reduction in the size, the average being under 60 mm. This difference in the figures, however, might be due in slight part to the greater number measured in 1904.

The size of the yearlings at the time of their movement varies more or less in different localities. In the Naha, in 1903, 943 specimens averaged 65 mm., with extremes of 48 and 100 mm.; in 1904, 2,714 specimens averaged 59 mm., extremes 47 to 115. (See diagram A.) In the Fraser River, as reported by Babcock, the average is 76 mm. Fifty-seven examples from the Wallowa River, Oregon, taken April 20, averaged 100 mm., with extremes of 99 and 132 mm. Besides these, in the same lot, were 6 females averaging 163 mm. (extremes 155 and 178 mm.), which were distinct in size and did not intergrade with the remainder. That they were not the dwarf form is shown by the large number of eggs in the ovaries, the large sockeye bearing always far more than the dwarf is known to contain.

The presence of these large individuals raises the question of a possible second winter's residence in the fresh water. Young sockeyea were found in the Wannuck up to 150 mm. and in the Karluk up to 221 mm., with the spring migrants. The Karluk fish intergrade with the smaller, indicating merely unusual growth. The only disturbing factor in the Karluk data is the fact that some of the larger of these young fish, taken June 25 at the mouth of the lake going up stream, show such enlargement of the testes as to indicate approaching sexual maturity. The largest male and the two females taken in the same lot show no unusual precocity and the ovaries indicate the large form. The maturing males may be the dwarf form, but it is more probable that they are precocious individuals of the ordinary type.

In the yearling sockeye the sexes run approximately equal. Of 1,550 of the 1904 catch examined, 51 per cent were males and averaged 0.2 mm. greater than the females in length, the sexes standing, respectively, 59.7 to 59.5 mm. It appears that the greater size of the male becomes early characteristic.

Migration Of Yearlings.

The migration of the yearlings seems to be wholly a matter of instinct. In 1903 the Naha reached a temperature of 40 F. about the middle of April. By the end of that month most of the ice was out of the lakes, but the temperature had not risen further. By

"On diagram read "yearlings" for "fingerlings." the middle of May, when the temperature of the lagoon had reached 45 F., though the upper river was still about 40, the young fish began leaving in large numbers. The run, however, after lasting about two weeks, fell off abruptly, before any marked rise in temperature had occurred. In 1904 ice had left the lakes very much earlier, but the temperatures were not notably higher the middle of May than in the previous year; yet on May 17 the movement was at full height and continued so till the end of the first week in June, when the water had reached a surface temperature of over 50. It then fell away little less abruptly than in the previous year. During this period the fish showed no corresponding increase in size as the season advanced, i. e., they maintained about the same average for the four weeks covering the main run, only the remnant stragglers late in June having increased in average length.

In natural spawning the first deposited spawn must be in no small part destroyed by the activities of late-coming fish. Of the eggs deposited after low temperatures obtain, the product of the earlier will perhaps to a certain extent be evened with the later hatching in that it will not develop rapidly during the winter, and with the rapidly warming water of spring the incubation value of each day augments to lessen the total number of days required in the development of the fry from the egg. Hence, while some fry may be ready to move with the opening of the river from ice, the maximum number will accrue gradually and fall away abruptly even though the spawning be more or less evenly distributed over a greater period, as appears to be the case in species migrating as fry. When the young feed for a period or season before migrating this effect will be obliterated by the superior ability of the larger of them to obtain food and hasten their growth.

That the migration of yearlings takes place in such manner that the average size of the migrants is about the same throughout the season is shown in the following table:

Lengths Ok M1grat1ng Yearl1ng Sockeyeh At Stat1on 2, Naha R1ver, 1904.

During the month occupied in the migrator-movement there should have occurred a growth of some 4 mm. in average length, but this in nowise appears, and it may be that the late-hatched vigorous fish whose superior feeding and digestive powers must have advanced them beyond less thrifty earlier-hatched are among the first to reach salt water.

In the British Columbia work it was shown that the movement took place in the Thompson bet ween the first of April and the middle of July, the run of fry being largest in April, with a temperature of 41, whereas in the Fraser, with an April average of 36, both fry and yearlings ran about one month later. The *M&y* temperatures of the two streams are about equal—46 for the. Thompson and 45 for the Fraser. In June they reached, respectively, 53 and 51. In the Wallowa River the movement apparently takes place in April; temperature unknown.

It would seem from these observations that migration begins when the water has-reached a temperature of about 40. At this time surface food begins to be plentiful, hence the necessity of seeking new feeding grounds would appear to be less than it is earlier in the season. But before any definite statement can be made regarding food influences it will be necessary to become familiar with the crustacean life of the lakes. In the fall, at least some of the principal crustacean forms are multiplying, yielding an increased food supply which might account for the continuance of crustacean feeders in the lakes. Surface food at that season decreases, hence the tarriers in the streams, as coho and king, must move on as winter approaches. That scarcity of food has some influence might be supposed from the usual paucity of aliment in the stomachs of moving fish. Occasionally there will be found a stomach partially filled, but they seldom contain more than a small part of the quantity ordinarily found in examples taken from the resident individuals in any waters. It is probable that the fish take only what presents itself without any searching on their part.

Floods seem to have little influence on the movement of yearlings beyond the possible temperature influence. Fry are apparently swept out by high water, movement near the mouth of the streams inclining to be heaviest on falling water. No catch of yearlings was made in daylight in the Naha where the water is clear, and though the catch was uninterrupted during the night it appeared to be heaviest in the evening, daybreak seeming again to accentuate the movement slightly. In the muddy waters of the Fraser the catch was continuous through the day. The apparatus used, however, would not be effective in clear water in daylight, and its results can not be taken as a sure indication of the time of movement. That there is little movement in day in clear water is highly probable, since none has been directly observed.

The exact behavior of the large schools of yearlings has been fully described by Mr. Babcock in the report for British Columbia, 1903. They were observed to move down the lake in the afternoons, running headfirst from the quiet waters of the lake into the current of the outlet. Seton Lake is 17 miles in length and about 1 mile in width. In this body of water there can be no perceptible current setting down the lake, since the winds would produce more tide than gravity; temperatures, while higher at the head than at the foot, will exhibit no sensible gradual increase after a short distance from the inflow of the cold streams. Yet these schools, apparently guided by instinct alone, approach the outlet directly. Were not the same phenomenon exhibited by migrating fry, as humpback, for example, it might be supposed that the year's residence in the lake has familiarized them with its geography.

Upon reaching a pronounced riffle, they "turn en masse and head upstream, circling and moving more or less rapidly in the more quiet stretches before venturing to approach the dam," i. e. , the main fall. Their timidity in approaching swift water was notable. Only with the waning light would the first few allow the current to carry them down, the movement, or rather passivity, gradually becoming more and more general. It will be remarked that in heavy runs the average size is slightly smaller. This would seem to indicate that fishes not otherwise quite ready to migrate are drawn out by the general movement. The hesitancy to encounter swift water is noticeable in the adult as well. Spaulding at Karluk remarked it as a prominent feature of the movement of spawners in the small streams, and schools often are noted standing in a swift current, seeming to hesitate to ascend or descend as the case may be. It would appear that this trait may have had no small influence in producing a resident form, though there is no reason to believe that the dwarf sockeyes as now known *(O. nerka Icennerlyi)* are the product of the regular form, i. e., only tardy young that have failed to migrate with their fellows, and thereby remained to reach sexual maturity in fresh waters. Their distinctive size, varying with waters inhabited, and the small number of eggs present in the ovary when yet little developed, mark them as at least a distinct race.

It has been reported" that by the damming of streams for producing reservoirs to supply San Francisco and Oakland with water, the salmon then in those streams were landlocked. As a result they remained in the reservoirs and reproduced. Ultimately, by reason of the confinement and its effects, they became dwarfed, decreasing from their original weight of 12 to 14 pounds to less than 1 pound at maturity.6 The continual breeding of this species *(0. tschawytscha),* in confinement in fresh water seems to produce dwarfing, even with abundance of food. At the Trocadero Aquarium, where they have

"Report Commissioner of Fisheries, California, 1870-77, p. 5 and f. 6 See report by W. N. Lockington, in Report Commissioner of Fisheries, California, 1878-79, p. 50.

been bred in fresh water for several generations, the 4-year fish weigh from 2 to 4£ pounds. These are from the Sacramento fish which average between 15 and 20 pounds. At the same time the number of eggs has diminished from a normal number of about 6,000 to only 1,300 to 1,400.

These examples demonstrate a possible effect of fresh-wrater residence. Dwarf sockeyes occur in such lakes as Alturas, Wallowa, Seton, Ozette, etc., in all of which fish may come and go at will. No other species of the genus breeds in lakes or exclusively in lake tributaries. It may be that the sockeye is in process of evolution from an anadromous form to a permanent fresh-water resident. Part of the young apparently possess the primal instinct to return to sea at once the first year, another and greater part have changed to become oneyear residents, and the smallest part have lost the to-ocean instinct entirely and remain to reach maturity in the lakes. Experiments as to the action of artificially reared young of the two races would be of the utmost interest and no little value to fish-culturists. The existence of marine and fresh-water forms of the same species is well known in Atlantic Salmonidae, and as well in other families. The effect of change of habitat in the two forms respectively has in no instance been worked out, and remains for solution, one of the most interesting and important problems in ichthyology and fish-culture.

KING SALMON. AGE AND SEASON OF MIGRATION.

The observations on the Sacramento River have demonstrated that the king salmon young in that stream for the most part leave the fresh water as soon as they are able to swim and feed. All the spawning occurs in the upper parts of the river and its tributaries, yet fry with unabsorbed yolk were sometimes taken only a short, distance above tidal influence." This same action was noted in the Karluk. On July 3 a trap which had been set overnight at the mouth of that river just above the lagoon took 1,300 fry, nearly all of which were king; there were only 4 humpback and 7 sockeye fry among the examples saved. As the collector did not differentiate species it is impossible to say whether 7 were all of the sockeye fry in the 1,300, or whether that number was only the natural proportion among the 180-odd specimens saved. The humpback being of striking appearance, however, it is probable the 4 saved were the entire catch of that haul. It should be stated that the haul also contained 5 sockeye yearlings, 25 coho fingerlings, a few sticklebacks, flounders, and young trout. No other sets of this trap were made; hence it is impossible to state "Rutter, Natural history of the quinnat salmon. Iiullclin U. S. Fish Commission, vol. xxn, 1902, p. 92.

what period the run of king fry occupied, but inasmuch as a few were taken in daylight, and the total number taken was so large, it would seem probable that the migration at that time was near its height. No fry of this species were taken in seine hauls made in the river May 22.

On the lower Sacramento the principal migration of the king fry occurs in March and April. Ice never forms on their breeding grounds, and they are free to travel as soon as they are able, which the temperature of the water and consequent time of hatching make possible at the above date. The adults reach the river in April, May, and June, and in August and September. They spawn in numbers from the middle of August to the end of September, and from the beginning of October until in December. The first eggs deposited begin to hatch about September, and fry begin to migrate about October, or even earlier, and continue throughout the winter, since no obstacle is offered by ice, and the fall and winter rains put the stream into the most favorable condition. The run is practically over by April 1 on the lower river. From that date on it will be noted that the examples taken gradually increase in size, showing them to be in a manner summer residents."

In the Karluk the adults first appear about the mouth of the river in May and continue in small numbers into August. They are known to spawn in the river below the lake late in August, or at approximately the same season as in California. The different time of migration of the fry is accounted for by the difference in average water temperature. In the Sacramento the eggs are deposited in water of a temperature of 56 to 46 F. , the winter temperature rarely reaching as low as 40. In the Karluk the lake surface in August varies between 40 and 50, or slightly above, and as the spawn of this species is deposited in the stream below the lake this may be taken to be the approximate temperature of the spawning beds. It is improbable that any great number enter the lake as adults to spawn in the lake tributaries. At an average temperature of 45 (it is probably less) during August and September eggs deposited in the latter part of August could not hatch before the middle of November. By this time it is probable that the temperature has dropped to freezing, and it is doubtful whether even the earliest eggs hatch before the advent of spring. The lake probably clears of ice and the water begins to warm up late in April or early in May. With the increased warmth, due to the long periods of day in that latitude, the fry would have developed at about the date noted, namely, late in June and early in July. As there is little rain at that season, there would seem to be no cause for the downstream movement except age (development) and instinct.

As in the Sacramento, it was found that a small number of young king salmon remain in the river until they reach the size of fingerlings. Five yearlings averaging 111 mm. total length were taken in Karluk Lake June 5; 2 females slightly smaller, June 23 and 30; 2 males, 115 mm., were taken in an upstream trap at the mouth of the river July 3, and 2 slightly smaller examples on the 5th. This would indicate that they were feeding in the river at this date. In a seine haul on the lagoon 4 males averaging 130 mm. and 4 females averaging 135 mm. were taken July 24, in company with large numbers of sockeye and king fry and a few coho and sockeye fingerlings (or yearlings) and small trout. It has not been noted that these feeding fingerlings migrate in schools, but Rutter has shown that in the Sacramento, with the growing scarcity of food in the fall and the opportunity offered by fall freshets, they gradually forsake their summer quarters.

The "summer residents" were also found in abundance in the Columbia River work of 1895. The altitude of these breeding waters and the proximity of snow tends to reduce the temperatures below those of the Sacramento, altitude doubtless effecting for them what latitude does for the Karluk. The bottom temperatures given for Alturas Lake can not be relied on, owing to the character of the instrument with which they were taken. It is probable that the bottom temperature at 150 feet is little over 40 F., as shown by later observations in Wallowa and other lakes. The falling air temperatures of the autumn must be closely followed by the water. The circulation in these lakes must be comparatively small and the cooling of the waters rapid..

Dr. Evermann's researches show that the lake temperatures, and consequently those of the spawning waters, fall rapidly after August. Since the king salmon deposits its eggs late in August and early in September, it is likely that the early freezing of the water arrests the development of the fry, so that they can not arrive at the migrating stage until some time in the spring. Biit, in so far as the temperatures taken in Idaho are somewhat above the corresponding observations in Karluk Lake, it is probable'that the downstream migration of the main schools would have been completed before the arrival of the investigating party in July. The size and growth of the fingerlings found exhibit a condition exactly analogous to that described by Rutter for the Sacramento and observed in a less degree for the Karluk.

EFFECT OF CHANGE FROM FRESH TO SALT WATER.

Rutter demonstrated that the king salmon fry is unable to sustain immediate transfer from fresh water to sea water. In addition to his experiments on the California salmon, he made a test at Karluk.

"Evennann, Bulletin U. S. Fish Commission, vol. xv1, 1896, p. 157.

August 2 about 600 fry and fingerlings were placed in a live-box 3 by 3 by 7 feet and towed from the river through the lagoon to the sea, a trip of 5 hours. About 50 died en route, 150 died during the following night, and all but 70 in the next 24 hours. These were probably all king salmon. The totals show that all under 2 inches died; 6 percent of the fingerlings up to 2$ inches lived; 94 per cent of the larger fingerlings lived. This result is singular enough when it is noted that the king salmon young migrating out of the river are but If inches in average length. Tt is inconceivable that they remain in the fresh-water end of the lagoon until they have added 50 per cent to their size. Two-inch fish were taken by Eigenmann in 1890 at Mare Island; 2i-inch examples were taken by the writer in 1898 in San Pablo Bay in brackish water. There is every reason to believe that fingerlings of the latter length under natural conditions are perfectly able to endure a standard salinity. The fact that this species breeds only in rivers of considerable volume insures to the young the opportunity of making the transition with the necessary gradualness. In this they differ from the frequenters of short streams, the fry of which species are doubtless able to endure a sudden entry into salt water.3

The tendency of the resident king fingerlings to advance upstream has been pointed out by Evermann in the report of the Columbia River inquiry. The same habit was noted by Rutter, and the presence of king salmon in the catches at Karluk Lake verifies the earlier observations, showing that the location of the breeding ground is not closely indicated by the presence of the young.

FOOD.

The food of this species is almost wholly insects, in large part from the surface. The yearlings mentioned above, taken in Karluk Lake, contained only insects, as did also the young taken at the mouth of the river; but the 8 taken in the lagoon contained amphipods in addition. These large fish must be yearlings. Their presence in the lake can be accounted for only on the assumption that the fry or fingerlings migrated into the lake the previous season, or that the yearlings ascend the stream in the spring and summer. Since their natural food would become scarce early in the fall it would seem to be improbable that they would remain in the fresh water, whereas the length of the river and the unnaturalness of an instinct that would impel female yearlings to ascend it from salt water lay that supposition open to serious question. They remain to be accounted aberrant individuals "Questions regarding the change from fresh to salt water, and vice versa, made by all the salmon, have been discussed in detail by Sumner (Bulletin U. S. Bureau of Fisheries, vol. xxv, 1905, p. 53-108) and by Greene (Bulletin U. S. Bureau of Fisheries, vol. xxiv, 1904, p. 429-156). that have obeyed neither the instinct to descend as fry nor that to seek the sea in self-preservation upon the approach of winter.

Migrating fry at the river mouth were largely empty, but a few contained insect remains. The small fingerlings taken in a seine haul in the lagoon also showed a purely insect diet. The lot taken by the trap at the river's mouth averaged about 42 mm. (37-53); those seined in the lagoon averaged 47 mm. (40-62), showing a growth of about 5 mm. since reaching brackish water perhaps not over a month previously. It was noted that late in July the number of these small fish seen about the margins of Karluk Lagoon had greatly decreased, indicating that the stay of the main body in brackish water is short.

COHO SALMON. EARLIEST MIGRATIONS.

As in case of the king salmon, a considerable number of coho young remain as summer residents in the streams of their birth or in the connecting lakes; but the greater part seek the sea as soon as they become free-swimming. In the trap at station 2, on the Naha, the fingerlings and yearlings taken largely exceeded the fry in number. Both were taken from the middle of May until in June—the migration period coinciding with that of the socke'e. It is possible that this migration is in large part influenced by the sockeye movement. When yearlings of the latter species travel at the surface the cohos of similar size may be impelled, to some extent, to school with them; but the general absence of yearlings in the lakes early in the summer indicates that the spring migration is instinctive and general for the species.

The fry reach the swimming stage somewhat later in the season than the sockeye. The eggs, though requiring a slightly shorter incubation period than those of the sockeye, are deposited much later in the fall. By means of a trap which was set in Steelhead Creek on Naha Bay in 1904 the migration was found to be heavy as early as May 19, water at 48. On this date over 1,100 fry were taken, the net spanning the entire stream. This run reached its maximum ten days later, when over 3,000 fry were taken in a single night. It continued, however, until sometime in July, when the temperature had reached 54. In this creek the humpback and the dog fry left in May, the coho from the middle of May through June, and the steelhead in July. These dates are approximate for these species in the Loring district.

FOOD AND HABITS.

The fry taken in the trap during the time from May to July 9 showed no appreciable increase in size, the catch average varying irregularly between 37 and 40 mm. Of 600 measured, 85 per cent were between 36 and 40—extremes 33 and 43 mm. A few fingerlings, less than 1 per cent, were taken-at the same time. The food at that time, in the few that contained any, was insects. The main movement was early in the evening, the lifting of the trap at 1.30 a. m. and 9.30 a. m. of the same day showing a catch of 2,015 between dusk (about 10 p. m.) and 1.30 a. m. and 50 during the morning twilight.

In the Karluk in 1903 the first specimens of coho fry were obtained May 22. At that time salmon fry and small fingerlings were said to be numerous in the little sloughs at the edge of grassy marshes where the current was slight. Over 1,000 were taken in a single haul of the seine. Of the 42 examples preserved from this haul only 2 were cohos, about 38 mm. long, 1 with insect food. Of the 17 fingerlings saved from the same haul 15 were cohos, 12 males averaging 68 mm. and 3 females averaging 52 mm., all feeding on insects and larva?. It should be noted that the small fingerling sockeyes taken in this haul contained crustaceans, some also insects and insect larva?, while the 2 yearling sockeyes contained only insects and larvae. Small fingerlings were taken in Karluk Lake July 27, 30, and 31, and as late as August 22. In all but 2 examples examined, which contained crustacea, the food was insects and insect larvae.

Coho young may be found in almost every brook of Alaska throughout the summer. They linger along the margins and in the pools, with no apparent seaward movement. As the adults penetrate all these small streams to spawn, the upstream movement of the young, if there be any, does not excite attention. They are resident in the lakes as well as in the tributary streams. With the fall rains these residents are swept out of the streams into the lakes or the sea in the same manner as the king.

In the summer of 1905 many coho fingerlings were taken in Yes Lake. August 22, 15, averaging 95 mm. in length

(63-122 mm.), were taken in a night haul. Two of these (13 per cent) contained sticklebacks, one having eaten 12, all less than 20 mm. in length; 66 per cent were feeding on flies, etc.; 13 per cent contained beetles, and 26 per cent snails; 13 per cent had eaten caddis larvae, and a like number other larva?. August 24, 55 were taken in night hauls of a shore seine, average length 85.6 mm., extremes 53-130. Of these, 91 per cent contained winged insects, as flies and ants; 42 per cent beetles; 14 per cent mites, eggs, etc.; 7 per cent sticklebacks; 7 per cent snails; and 5 per cent caddis larvae. September 10, 88 were secured in the same manner, average length 83 mm., extremes 51-120. Of these, 44 per cent contained winged insects and the same number caddis larvae, 20 per cent beetles, 11 per cent mites, etc., about 2 per cent sticklebacks, 5 per cent snails, and 7 per cent other larvae than caddis. It will be noted that the average size of the latter lot is slightly smaller, but the decrease is not sufficient to indicate a movement of the larger individuals out of the lake. A more significant fact is the growing scarcity of surface food and greater amount of bottom material—the caddis found in their stomachs.

As early as April 6 (1903) coho yearlings of 145 to 165 mm. were gilled at the Fortmann Hatchery in Heckman Lake at the mouth of the river. They were attracted by the waste eggs thrown in the river.

May 17, 1903, 11 males taken at station 2 averaged 119 mm., and 8 females 112; May 24 of the following year 12 males averaged 125 and 18 females 123. If these may be regarded as typical there appears to be a growth of about 50 per cent between September and May, or about twice that which from similar data was estimated for the sockeye. The yearling cohos taken in the Naha were found to eat the young salmon fry whenever taken with them in the nets. That they sometimes were able to prey upon them in a natural state was evidenced by the presence of digested fry in some examples that were seined in Roosevelt Lagoon in May.

September 12, 1897, the writer seined a number of young cohos at the mouth of Klawak River. No other fish except sticklebacks were noted. Of the 71 cohos saved the 37 males averaged 85 mm. in length (50-125); the 34 females averaged a small fraction of a millimeter greater (47-135). At this time the hatchery was operating and sockeyes were spawning in the lake tributaries above. Many of these young cohos contained salmon eggs. A more common food was a large maggot, probably the blowfly larva5 from dead fish along the stream. One stomach contained 2 leeches, and many of the smaller had insects. Examples taken with a hook in brackish water at the Klawak cannery wharf contained insects and a few beach crustaceans; 50 examples from the lake, October 14, 1905, averaged about 75 mm. These were taken with a dip net and do not give the average size of lake residents of that date. (See also record in salt water, p. 53.) Like the king fingerling the coho is readily taken with a hook, either with a fly or bait, salmon spawn being especially attractive in season. During the spawning season the coho in a few places may do some damage to the sockeye eggs. Large numbers are attracted to the scene of the hatchery work at Loring by the washings from the freshly spawned eggs. They were nowhere noted in any number on the natural beds.

As the result of the wide diversity of spawning regions, the coho may be said to possess three movements seaward, first as fry, second as fall fingerlings in the same manner as the king, and third as yearlings, lake winter residents leaving in the spring with the sockeyes. This may be true also of the king salmon, but it is not believed, from the observations on the Columbia, that the king spawns above the lakes ordinarily, hence only the wandering young would winter in them.

DOG SALMOfJ.

The dog-salmon young, so far as known, all leave the fresh water as soon as they are able to swim. The records of the occurrence of larger individuals in streams have not been authenticated. The dog-salmon fingerlings reported in the rivers of Washington by Gilbert and Evermann" on later examination were found to be cohos. A similar find by Davis6 likewise proved erroneous.

This species breeds in the Naha in too limited numbers to permit observations of value. Fry were taken in only two instances at station 2. A few were taken at station 1 the middle of April, and again in Gibson and Emma creeks the middle of May. They were found in abundance, however, running out of the creeks of Deep (Moser) Bay, April 30, temperature 37, many of them still with remnants of yolk. A few were found in Steelhead Creek after May 7 and up to June 6. In the main their fresh-water habit seems identical with that of the humpback.

Early in June, 1903, immense schools of small fingerling dog salmon were seen leaving the Karta River. Examples taken on the 8th of that month about the margins of the upper Kasaan Bay average about 40 mm. They were feeding on insects. It was reported by the workmen building the Alaska Packers' Association trap at that point that shoals of these young could be seen at times well out in the bay, where they were pursued by larger fish, apparently Dolly Varden trout. The great number of adult dog salmon spawning in the Karta River makes this easily credible.

In the Karluk lagoon, 1903, fry and small fingerlings were observed in large numbers May 12-14. They lay close inshore by the spit, moving about in schools, but not going out with the tide. Some of these still contained yolk, others were feeding on insect larva1, amphipods, and surface material. Slightly larger young were taken in the lagoon June 9-12, feeding on crustaceans and insects. June 18 they were noted as abundant outside on Karluk Beach, 6 taken averaging 50 mm. in length; they were feeding on insects, crustaceans, and small cottoids. July 24 neither dog nor humpback young were present among the examples taken in a seine haul in the lagoon, all apparently having sought the sea. (See p. 52.)

"Gilbert and Evermann, Bulletin U. S. Fish Commission, vol. xiv, 1894. p. 198. b Davis, Pacific Fisherman, vol. i, no. 4, May, 1902, p. 9. 10731—07 i
HUMPBACK SALMON.

The fry of the humpback salmon leave the fresh water with the breaking up of ice. In 1903 they were first taken April 12 at station 1 on the Naha, but the number secured, 240, indicates that this was not the beginning of the run, though all the lakes were still covered with ice. The number migrating increased from this date to the end of the month, and they were found leaving the lagoon throughout May. During this time there was no increase in average size, the fry apparently leaving as rapidly as they attained sufficient strength. They traveled almost wholly by night, the heaviest movement apparently being on the first of falling water after a rise. At these times the average size was slightly less than at others. On April 19 a trap set near station 3 took over 1.500 fry. There is but a very small spawn ng ground below Jordan Lake above the point where tjiis net was set, and it is thought that the larger part of the run indicated by this catch had passed through Jordan Lake under the ice. The average size was a trifle greater than that of the fry taken at the same time at station 1, wholly because of fewer undersized fish.

Very few Tiumpback fry were seen at Karluk, a few were taken at the mouth of the river May 11, and again July 3, but at no time did they appear abundant. One example occurred in an experiment testing for endurance of salt water and was found to survive the test.

While the young humpbacks are in fresh water, feeding is only incidental. A few have been found to contain remains of insects, larva;, and crustacea. As with the dog salmon and coho, the descent from the small creeks in which many are hatched makes it necessary that they be able to stand a quick change to salt water. In carrying a number from the trap in fresh water to the lower Naha Bay it could not be observed that immediate immersion in salt water caused them the least inconvenience.

TROUT lSTEELHEAD?) AND CHARR.

The first trout fry appear in Steelhead Creek about July 1. On that date in 1903, 255 were taken in the trap, and on the following day 295. About the same number were present again in 1904, 283 being taken on July 9. While no further trials of the trap were made in 1903 the fry were noted to continue in the creek in large numbers until swept out by the fall rains about the middle of September. During this period their abundance was almost incredible when viewed with regard to the number of adults seen in the spawning season.

In the lower Karta River July 26, 1903, trout fry were very numerous. At this time the temperature was 64 and the stream very low. Along the sandy bars in places the receding of the water had left pools in wh ch large numbers of fry were imprisoned. The temperature in these pools was much higher than in the stream, and in many cases the water had evaporated, leaving the fry to die. All of them were swept out by the first rise.

At Karluk, August 29, 1903, in a small stream tributary to the small lake east of the main lake, Spaulding noted the occurrence of fry imprisoned in the same manner. From the date and place it is believed that, these were trout fry. No examples were preserved. Small fingerlings and fry of trout may be seen during the late summer almost as widely distributed as the coho.

So far as observed the food of the trout fingerling is insects. The observations were made on July 11 in a pool about 6 to 18 inches deep at the foot of the fall in Flume Creek, where numbers of both trout and coho young fingerlings were resident for several weeks. The coho were schooling near the surface; the trout inclined rather to scatter and occupy the bottom. One trout was observed to take a position on a rock, from which it would dart for food to either side and forward for some 20 inches, returning each time to the same resting place. During the eight or ten minutes it was observed, it made over twenty trips, once attacking and driving away a brother fingerling that tried to take a place upstream and cut off the food supply. The trout rarely came to the surface, striking mostly at submerged drifting particles. Upon return to the pool two hours later the fingerling was found to be gone.

The fry of the charr occur in very much smaller number. A slight migratory movement was noted in Steelhead Creek in 1904. Two were taken in the trap May 29, 16 on June 5, and on the 13th 30, the last observed. Their habit is to burrow in the gravel in the small streams. In these places their protective coloration and agility permit them readily to elude observation. No notes were made on the food of these young.

Fingerlings of all sizes of trout and charr were taken in the trap at various times, but no indication of any migratory movement appeared. Both species pass indifferently to and from salt water. The seaward movement of the fry is unquestionable, but individuals that remain in the streams after the fry period are doubtless governed only by convenience in obtaining protection and food. In the pools called Trout Ponds on Trail Creek only cutthroats and' charrs were taken with a hook. These never exceeded a certain size, about 8 inches, though both male and female ripe cutthroats were taken May 30. In the brook below larger individuals were taken, a ripe female cutthroat being secured April 25. No steelheads were noted in Trail Creek, but a few trout fry may be found there. In Steelhead Creek only rainbow and Dolly Varden trout are taken below the falls, but in the lake above the falls cutthroats are abundant. These falls are probably now impassable at all stages of water, and it is hardly to be believed that fry of the trout in the lakes help to account for the abundance of trout fry in the stream. It is to be observed that their numbers decrease toward the upper reaches, so that for some distance below the falls few are seen, and none in the few yards of the stream between the lake and the head of the falls.

SEA HABITS OF YOUNG SALMON. NOTES AFFORDED BY COLLECTIONS AND RECORDS. THE SOCKKYE.

The sea habitat of the young sockeye so far has not been studied. The only observations available are the results of occasional and irregular seine hauls made by the *Albatross* parties at various times, accompanied usually by no notes regarding exact locality or associated forms. These scant collections throw little light upon the sea habits or habitat. The gear used was capable only of taking examples in comparatively shallow water, close inshore, on smooth beaches. Larger examples would scarcely be t aken under these conditions even if present in the same waters, and smaller fry would not be held by the web ordinarily used in the vessel's seines.

The smallest specimens in the collection are 8 examples averaging 41 mm. , from Sumner Harbor, taken July 2, 1896. This harbor is a small bay northeast of the town of Unalaska. It receives a small creek, the outlet of a lake. The fry were taken in company with coho fry and fingerlings. The sockeyes were feeding on crustacea, the cohos on both crustacea and insects. If they were taken in the bay, they were doubtless recent migrants from the lake. These sockeyes differ somewhat from the more southerly specimens in having shorter and less numerous gillrakers—about 10-17; in coloration they resemble some of the examples from Karluk, the parr marks being longer and more bar-like than in those from Southeast Alaska.

A number of fingerlings from Wood River, Bristol Bay, taken July 23, 1903, averaged about 41 mm. in length. The stomachs were filled with small crustaceans and insects. Wood River has little fall from the lake which it drains, and in spring tides is affected as far as the lake. No notes accompany the specimens, so they are of little biological significance. They seem to differ from the Southeast Alaska examples of similar size in being of less tapering outline and having a smaller eye. Six yearlings, average 98 mm., are in the same lot, with the same food present in the stomachs. The main run from the Kvichak River was reported to Mr. John N. Cobb, of the Bureau of Fisheries, as occurring from the first to the middle of June, fish from 3$ to 4 inches in length. These are taken for eating by the Chinese at the cannery. Some are said to be pink-meated.

The next smallest examples in the salt-water collections are 12 from Alert Bay, British Columbia, taken June 5, 1895, probably from the beach near the cannery. With these arc a number of small dog fingerlings of about 40 mm. and possibly a few humpback. Many of the specimens are in poor condition and not positively identifiable. The sockeyes average 62 mm. (53-68). Their food is all pelagic material, small adult copepods, ostracods and amphipods, crab larvae, and a worm-like marine form—*Sagitta*. The other species were also feeding on crustacea.

From Nikolski, Bering Island (Komandorskis), there are 5 yearlings taken July 3, 1895; 2 males, 121 and 130 mm., 3 females, 133 to 135 mm.; all with amphipods in the stomachs.

From Kiska Island, June 7, 1894, 1 male, 196 mm., containing copepods, and 2 females, 230 and 245 mm., with stomachs empty. These are said to have been taken in a small lake, but data for this are incomplete. They are apparently not dwarfs.

From Isanotski Straits, at the extremity of the Peninsula of Alaska, 5 examples were obtained July 15, 1894; 3 males, 123 to 135 mm., and 2 females, 132 and 143 mm. The only stomach left in the specimens *by* the collector contained small crustacea, schizopods, and amphipods. These fishes w'ere all infested with a parasitic roundworm occurring in masses in the region of the air-bladder. They are also noteworthy for the shortness of the gillrakers. These (on the right side) average less than 33 in number, the longest equal to about the distance between 6, or spanning 5 interspaces. The specimens from Nikolski average 34, with a length equal to about 5 interspaces. Those from Kiska run high, averaging 36 in the 3 examples at hand. Dundas Bay specimens, in a count of 12 somewhat smaller individuals, give an average number of 33 + with average length a little less than 5 interspaces, whereas Karluk fish, in 10 examples taken June 8, 1903, show an average number of 35 4-and a length equal to nearly 9j interspaces.

The examples from Dundas Bay were taken July 24, 1903, in a seine haul on the tide flats with mud and sand bottom. With them occurred dog and humpback fingerlings of about the same size, perhaps in the same school. The individuals saved are 6 males, average '80.6 mm. (71-91), and 6 females, average 77. 7 (73-85). They were feeding on crustaceans, insects, and insect larvaa.

At Uganuk young salmon are taken in large numbers in seine hauls for sand launces. Of 25 pounds of these small fishes taken in this manner June 15, 1903, 36 per cent were young salmon, mainly sockeyes, but in addition some cohos; 4 per cent were young herrings; the remaining 60 per cent were sand launces, or, as they are known locally, candlefish *(Ammodytes)*. The sockeyes of this lot whose stomachs were examined contained crustaceans, a few with fragments of insects also; several had small herring fry. Seventy-two males averaged 82.1 mm. in length (47-105); 70 females averaged 81.3 mm. (48-110).

It is a curious fact that in these collections, where there are large numbers of apparently regular-sized examples, usually the males are found to average slightly the larger, whereas in cases of only a few large examples the females almost always exceed the males in size.

At Karluk young salmon are found abundantly in the waters in which seining for the cannery is carried on. It is said these yearlings sometimes rush through the seines in clouds, and even in the largemeshed seines numbers are drawn ashore with the adults. From the catch on June 8, 1903, were saved 67 sockeyes, averaging 181 mm. (123-207). These were feeding on small crustacea; of 20 examined none had fry of any sort in the stomach. The distribution of food was peculiar in that individuals were feeding almost exclusively on a given form. For example, one was fdled with ostracods, others had but few; some had almost nothing but copepods, others as exclusively amphipods; many, however, had such a mixture as would be expected. This seems to indicate that the crustaceans form schools to a certain extent, either in zones or otherwise, which enables the fish, acting as a townet, to obtain more or less nearly pure masses of a given form. Among the specimens saved from this haul other than sockeyes were only 2 cohos. One of these had eaten a young cottoid of 18 mm. length.

On July 3 from a similar haul were saved 30 specimens; 12 males averaging 136 mm. (122-156), and 18 females averaging 139 mm. (125-164). Some of these were empty, most had been feeding on small crustaceans, several contained in addition small coiled shells (pteropods), and 2 had small blennies and sticklebacks in some number. One coho occurred in this lot.

July 24 young salmon were very abundant in Karluk Lagoon. A seine haul, with a 75-foot seine, covering about 250 square yards, took over 2,000 salmon, 30 to 150 mm. in length, and a few small trout and charrs. It is noteworthy that in this lot there seem to have been no humpbacks or dogs, whereas among specimens taken at the same time on the outer side of the spit, in the cannery seine, no sockeyes were saved. Whether this was a peculiarity of the distribution at that time or whether it arose from some other reason it is impossible to state. It is known that the collector did not closely differentiate the various species. The young sockeyes taken in the lagoon varied from 30 to 145 mm. in length. The smaller are doubtless from the hatchery, the yearlings may be from the lake; all were feeding on crustacea and insects, the smaller fish more on insects and their larva?, the larger on crustacea, mainly an amphipod. In several of each size were masses of intestinal worms.

It is stated that small salmon are seen in the seines throughout the canning season, but mainly in the earlier part. It will be noted that the larger specimens were obtained in June, and that after July 3 no collection of sockeyes was made from the cannery seines. It may be that the continual hauling in time frightens them away; but it seems more reasonable to believe that with increasing age they move farther out from shore. The vast numbers observed in June must be the yearling migrants from the lake. As to what becomes of the fry of the same season after reaching salt water, there is no clue, and can be none until search is made for them with small-meshed 'nets.

The only other specimens in the collection of interest in this connection are 2 males of 91 mm. and 5 females 84 to 104 mm., average 92.4 mm., taken in Karta Bay June 26, 1897. These contained mainly insects; some had also crustacea, and one had a few young flatfish.

THE KING SALMON.

It is a significant fact that in the collections at hand there occurs but one young king salmon taken in salt water. It would seem there should have been some in the Karluk Beach collections if the species is accustomed to tarry near its parent stream. They are sometimes taken in San Francisco Bay and the region outside the straits, but none of these examples have become part of the Bureau's collection. They have been reported also from the region of Killisnoo, Alaska. The example mentioned is a 215 mm. male, which was taken with the cohos (see below) at the Loring cannery wharf August 2, 1904. As this was preserved for a coho, it is possible that others of the 45 mentioned below were of this species.

THE COHO.

The young coho in salt water is more easily observed than the other species. It readily takes the hook, and apparently is less timid than the others in approaching surface and shore. In 1904 45 were taken at the Loring cannery wharf August 2. They averaged 190 mm. (158-226). On July 10 at the same place about 30 were taken. No measurements were made except of the largest, which was 138 mm. On August 2, 1905, a scattered school came about the *Albatross* while anchored at the extreme head of Yes Bay; 26, averaging 202 mm. (152-237), were taken with a hook over the ship's side. Only a few, 6 or 8, would appear at once, and they took the hook baited with bits of meat, etc., very shyly in the perfectly clear water. Most of the stomachs contained offal from the ship's messes; 5 contained fishes up to 65 mm. in length, all that could be identified being sand launces; 2 contained young sticklebacks, one of them 10 individuals; 2 had isopods, and only 3 had taken insects from the surface. Another example taken later, a male of 265 mm., contained 4 small herring.

At Karluk young cohos are occasionally taken in the cannery seines; two, 180 mm. long, preserved from the catch of June 8, contained 2 species of amphipods and one a young cottoid; one, 158 mm., preserved from the seine July 3, was an empty female; July 24, another, 175 mm. long, contained *Ammodytes*. As will be seen, these records indicate the presence of very few young cohos about Karluk Beach. The general collections of the *Albatross* afford the following data: A number of cohos were taken at Karta Bay with larger sockeyes, and smaller dog salmon on June 26, 1897. Of the specimens preserved 8 males average about 80 mm. (56-100), and 14 females average nearly 100 mm. (80-140). They were feeding mainly on insects and crustacea.

At Thorne Bay, July 5, of a number of small cohos together with a few dog salmon, seined probably at the mouth of the river, 24 males averaged about 55 mm. and 50 females about 56 mm., the high average of the latter being due to the presence of a few slightly larger individuals (extremes, males 45-65 mm., females 45-78 mm.). The stomachs examined contained insects for the most part; a few had small crustaceans and 2 had flatfishes.

At Port Alexander, July 3, 1903, many young cohos were taken in the seine; 4 males and 2 females were preserved; average about 150 mm. They were feeding on young herring and sand launces, also larval crabs and amphipods.

Of the specimens saved from Uganuk, June 15, 1903, 5 are males, averaging 138 mm., and 8 females, 130 mm. All but 3, which were empty, were feeding on young herring, each containing from 1 to 5 individuals. (See p. 51-52.)

At Unalaska 6 examples, taken July 23, 1888, average 148 mm., contained insects, crustaceans, grubs, and in one case a small fish like a salmon fry. One humpback fingerling was in this lot.

Twelve examples, taken at Sumner Harbor July 2, 1896, averaged about 60 mm. and were feeding on insects and crustacea. They were in company with the smaller sockeyes. (See p. 50.)

Isolated examples in the collection, not worthy of fuller notice, are: 1, Kilisut Harbor, July 1, 1903; 5, Tribune Bay, May-17, 1894; 3, Union Bay, British Columbia, June 22, 1903; 3, Cleveland Passage, July 13, 1903; 1, Pavlof Harbor, July 25, 1903; 1, Humboldt Harbor, Shumagin Islands, July 31, 1888; 3, New Morzhovoi, July 17, 1894, and 2, Kiska Island, June 7, 1894.

From the above data it is seen that the cohos remain for some months about the shores near the streams whence they issue. They may be found about the mouths of the streams in brackish water perhaps soon after their descent of the stream. It may be they remain about the streams for a time to accustom themselves to the salt water, but this is not evident in case of the fry. The sea-run examples are readily distinguished by the silvery appearance and usually by the greater depth of" body which follows habitual distension of the stomach. In some cases, while near in shore, insects appear to continue a staple article of diet, as in the fresh water. The cohos feed less on crustacea than the sockeyes, perhaps inhabiting slighter depths; correlated to this is the abundance of small fishes found in their stomachs—sticklebacks in brackish water and herring and sand launces in more open regions.

From the catches at Naha and Yes bays it would seem that the cohos continue to school after reaching salt water. The results of the seine hauls indicate that the different species of salmon school together, or at least in the same waters.

DOG AXD HUMPBACK SALMON.

On May 29, 1903, a small school of salmon, about 50 individuals, was seen along the shore about 1 mile below Naha Bay. Seven of these were secured—5 humpbacks 42 mm., and 2 dog slightly larger. The former were feeding on small crustacea and pteropods, the latter on crustacea and insect larvae.

On July 1 and 2 a few dog salmon fingerlings were taken in the net at station 2. These may have been either fishes that had remained in Roosevelt Lagoon since early spring, or stragglers from the bay coming in on high tide. Ten were males, averaging 56 mm., and 4 females, averaging 62. Those with food had been taking insects. (See also p. 47.)

At Karluk June 18 the fry of both dog and humpback salmon were abundant along the beach. Six preserved examples of the dog average about 50 mm., and contained insects, crustaceans, and small cottoid fry. Thirteen humpbacks saved average about 47 mm.; of the 6 larger ones examined 4 contained crustaceans, the other 2 nothing.

July 24 there were saved from the cannery seines 5 dog-salmon young, averaging 83 mm. (70-100), which contained a few insects and small fishes (blennies), but mainly crustaceans. Also 47 humpback young, averaging 77 mm. (60-95), the main food in which was copepods, but in addition were found flies, insect larvae, amphipods, and in a few cases small fry, probably *Lumpenus*, up to 18 mm. in length; 1 stomach contained 22 of these. Only the following collections were made by the *Albatross*:

In Alert Bay, British Columbia, June 5, 1895,.about 50 dog salmon small fingerlings were taken, along with a number of small sockeyes; these averaged about 40 mm. and contained only small crustacea.

In Admiralty Inlet, Whidby Island, on June 30, 1903, many young dog salmon were taken in a shore seine on gravel bottom. Of these 13 of each sex were preserved, the males averaging 09 mm. (83-117), females, 98 mm. (78-122). In none of the 9 examined were any fry found. They were feeding wholly on plankton material, crustacea, principally amphipods, and *Sagitta*. They appear to have been schooling alone.

In Otter Bay, Pender Island, British Columbia, 11 dog salmon were preserved from the collection of May 31, 1895. These averaged a little over 70 mm. and contained crustacea.

June 29, 1897, 4 dog salmon, 2 of each sex, averaging about 50 mm., were taken at Loring, it is believed in a seine haul on the seining beach of Roosevelt Lagoon. They contained only insects. These specimens, considered in connection with those obtained at station 2, noted above, point toward a continuance of some of the 3-oung of the dog salmon in brackish water for a period and suggest the desirability of investigating such waters with suitable gear. A haul was made in Roosevelt Lagoon on the night of October 1, 1905, but no salmon were obtained.

At Thome Bay, July 5, 1897, many dog-salmon young were taken in seine hauls on the beach just below the river; 64 of the specimens are males, averaging about 65 mm. (42-82), and 84 are females about 2 mm. longer (44-83). The food in those examined was crustacea, mainly ostracods. A few smaller ones taken in the river mouth were feeding on insects. In Karta Bay, June 26, 1897, dog, coho, and sockeye young were taken in the same hauls. Of the first, 19 males, about 60 mm. average, and 10 females, about 53 mm., were preserved. They were feeding mainly on insects and amphipods; a few contained small flatflsh, 1 being filled with them.

In Dundas Bay, July 24, 1903, many young salmon—sockeye, dog, and humpback—;were seined on the tide flats. The specimens of dog salmon are 4 males, about 75 mm., and 5 females, 82 mm. long. They were feeding on crustacea; a few had eaten insects and larvas in addition. The 3 humpback, 2 males and 1 female, average about 80 mm.; food the same as the other species. The 3 species were apparently schooling and feeding together.

In Pavlof Harbor, July 25, 1903, the seine was hauled at the mouth of a small stream in deep water, gravel beach. Many young dog salmon, a few cohos, sand launces, and other small fish were taken. The specimens of the first preserved are 4 males, about 100 mm. long, and 7 females, slightly smaller. Their food was crustacea, except, in one instance, a few flies.

At New Morzhovoi, July 17, 1894, 34 dog salmon young were preserved. These average about 80 mm. in length. The stomachs contain crustacea and gastropods; only 1 had insects. These specimens show the peculiar segregation of food noted in some sockeyes at Karluk (p. 52); some had eaten almost exclusively large copepods, others ostracods, and yet others a peculiar *CapreUa-likc* form.

Four specimens from Isanotski Straits, July 15, 1894, show no peculiar features.

At Sucia Island, May 6, 1894, 3 humpbacks and 1 dog salmon were taken, the former 47 mm. and the latter 54; food, crustacea.

At Metlakatla, July 10, 1903, 2 humpbacks were taken, 64 mm. in length. One was empty, the other contained flies.

Single specimens of humpback fingerling are recorded from Kodiak, August 14, 1888, and Unalaska, July 23 of the same year. The first, a female 113 mm. long, contained small fry and a few flies; the last, a male slightly larger, crustaceans.

CONCLUSIONS FROM AVAILABLE DATA.

From the above notes it may be concluded that many young sockeyes, after reaching saltwater as yearlings early in the spring, remain, in company with other young salmon, for a few months about the shores near the mouths of the streams from which they are derived; that during this time they feed principally upon the small crustaceans which are found from the surface to an unknown depth and, like the crustacean forms found in the lakes, have a diurnal movement from and to the surface. In tows made by the *Albatross* in the open ocean it has been found that many of these forms tend to be most abundant at the surface about dark, again decreasing in number within an hour or so. Whether the period repeats again at daylight was not tested. Surface tows in daylight made in Yes Bay and Behm Canal during July, August, and September, 1905, showed an almost entire absence of food material. At the same time it was found at depths of 20 to 75 fathoms and greater, the deeper the more abundant. It is known that this pelagic life is ultimately dependent upon the shore for food supply. The open sea far distant from land contains little life, unless it be conveyed by currents originating near land. The narrow and deep channels of Southeast Alaska furnish a superior environment for plankton life; to the wholly free-swimming forms, such as copepods, ostracods, etc., there is added the innumerable progeny of the littoral forms, such as crabs, worms, mollusks, and shore-spawning fishes.

ABUNDANCE OF FOOD.

As a test of the abundance of this salmon food material, during the summer of 1905 numerous hauls were made throughout Yes Bay and into Behm Canal. Yes Bay is a long, narrow inlet less than one-half mile in width and over 4 miles in length, the depth varying from 50 feet at the head to over 50 fathoms at the mouth. It receives several small creeks at the head and the main stream from Yes Lake, about midway between the two extremities. During the summer months the surface temperatures vary between 55 and 60, the lower nearer the mouth. The surface densities depend almost wholly upon the precipitation. During ordinary weather the head of the bay, from the pushing up of the dense bottom layers of water by the tides, acquires about half the density of sea water; midway, on account of the volume from the main stream from Yes Lake, the density is reduced to about one-fourth that of sea water, increasing to one-third or more as the mouth of the bay is approached. During freshets the surface density is much reduced, the water becoming practically fresh at times. The bottom temperatures vary from about 50 at the head in 50 feet of water to 44 in 330 feet at the mouth, with corresponding densities of about 1.018—or nearly three-fourths the density of sea water—to 1.0235, or closely approximating standard density. The tows exhibit a very scant population of food forms in the upper bay, with a gradual increase as the mouth is approached and a sudden rise upon entrance to the main channel outside. In the fresher waters jellyfishes predominate; with increasing density and depth the crustaceans increase in number.

This whole subject of the distribution of pelagic forms is of fundamental importance in the study of the sea habits of the salmon. With the pelagic forms, of course, must be considered also the shore forms, such, for instance, as the common amphipods (beach lice), which may be found under stones at low water; perhaps, also, certain mollusks, etc. The factors of temperature, density, light, depth of bottom, proximity of shore, set and velocity of currents, influence of land drainage, etc., require to be carefully studied. As yet nothing has been attempted in Alaskan waters toward the solution of these problems.

It will be noted that the Karluk sockeyes taken in salt water in June are of greater average size than those taken on subsequent dates at the same place. Further, that the average size of the June specimens is about twice that of the migrants from the Naha taken only a few weeks, earlier at Loring. If these Karluk sockeyes are accounted yearlings of average size for the locality, which have left the lake not earlier than April, more likely in May, they either have increased very rapidly in size since reaching salt water or were much larger than Naha yearlings at the time of migration. But for the uniformity of size it would seem more probable that the specimens procured are the selected larger examples, the smaller escaping through the meshes of the seine. There is the possibility that these larger individuals were fry that reached salt water the previous summer, and that the absence of smaller specimens in the collections is due merely to the escape of the fry and fingerling migrants of the same season through the large meshes of the selne. That yearlings from Karluk Lake are larger than those of the same age from the small lakes of Southeast Alaska may well be believed in view of the larger size of examples noted in Wallowa and

Alturas lakes and the Fraser River.

The dog-salmon young, cited above, vary from a little over 40 mm. to 120 mm.; the humpback show approximately the same figures. These are unquestionably of the fry that reached salt water in March and April just previous. The catches date about three months later. This indicates an increase of about 100 per cent in that length of time, or about twice the rate of growth of the sockeyes that remain in fresh water. In other words, the species (or individuals) that reach salt water as fry make about the same growth in the first three months that the lake residents (sockeyes) make in twelve. The comparison of fall catches of cohos and sockeyes in the lakes shows the former to exceed the latter greatly in size, but this is only a natural result of the coho's greater size from the fry stage to the adult. In the case of the humpback, however, the fry is scarcely larger than that of the sockeye, and the adult somewhat smaller. Its more rapid growth can be attributed only to the abundance of food in salt water and the nature of the fish. The sockeye young which were taken in salt water must be yearlings. Owing to the lateness of the migration of that species it is impossible for them to have attained such size in the time since they could have reached salt water as fry of that same season.

It will be seen that in general the four species of salmon are closely associated in sea habit. While small they remain much of the time close inshore, to some extent feeding on the insects that fall on the water or are carried down by the streams. The greater part of the food, however, is the various crustacean forms, though the small fry of marine species make up no small part, particularly of the coho's food. With increasing age the salmon doubtless move into deeper water. If the habit of preying on small fishes continues and grows with the increase of size, it would seem that the young salmon would be remarked in pursuit of the schools of young herring, sand launces, and such forms that abound in the bays and coast waters. No note of this has been recorded. Occasional catches of slightly larger fish are made from time to time, possibly fish of the second year. Such cohos are well known in Puget Sound, and a run of some small salmon was observed in Naha *Bay* during the winter of 1896-97. But unless such fish in large numbers approached the surface of some small body of water near a settlement, they would scarcely attract attention though the channels were teeming with them.

The salt-water habits of young trout and charrs are entirely unknown.

RETURN OF ADULTS TO FRESH WATER.
From the yearling stage to the adult little is known of any of the salmons, and nothing of the sockeye. There are reports of grown fish of that species taken in the winter in various places, as in the vicinity of Karluk and near Union Bay, Cleveland Peninsula; but the identification of these catches has not been authenticated. The only pertinent fact regarding their place of residence after leaving the vicinity of the parent streams, if they leave it, is that the presence of adult fish is first noted at the time when they are apparently rounding some point in their progress from more open water. Such places are Point Iliggins, at the entrance to Behm Canal; Capo Chacon, at the lower end of Clarence Straits, and Otter and Sheringham points, on Juan de Fuca Straits. Karluk River is apparently approached directly from the open straits.

APPROACH OF SCHOOLS..

The presence of salmon can be noted only by their habit of leaping from the water as they approach the land. It is often possible *hy* this means not only to recognize the presence of a school, but also to distinguish the species. In jumping, salmon do not leave the water with their ventral surface downward, as do flying-fishes. They always jump sidewise with one side at an acute angle to the water surface. Sockeyes seldom entirely clear the water, but let the tail drag for some distance, fall on the side, and then perhaps skim the water for a short space. They may make two or three successive jumps, apparently at random and in varying directions. Cohos usually leave the water entirely, falling back on the caudal peduncle held rigid with the fin directed upward. The tail may then drag through the water a short distance till the fish falls on its side and disappears. The humpbacks jump very agilely and characteristically. They leap clear of the water, shaking the tails vigorously while in the air, sometimes turning completely with a corkscrew motion. On falling they strike on the side.

The cause of this jumping has been much discussed. It was noted that a school of kings feeding in Xaha Bay in December, 1903, jumped in much the same manner as fish on the way to the spawning grounds, but apparently not so frequently, probably because of the small number of individuals under observation. The sockeye travels in large and compact schools when approaching the spawning regions, and the jumping should be easily accounted for in the natural playfulness of groups of animals or the struggle for preferred position. Stomachs of netted fish often contain salmon scales and teeth, the latter frequently the individual's own. But these are doubtless swallowed during the struggles in the net and not by reason of previous combats.

Under certain conditions the schools exhibit little tendency to jump. In 1903 large numbers of sockeyes entered Karluk River without such announcement. Of course it is not known whether this species feeds in schools in salt water, or whether it is only the approach of sex maturity that impels the gathering into schools. From the arrangement of the gillrakers, and the few observations made on feeding fish, it may be surmised that the larger part of their nutriment is derived from pelagic crustacea and associated forms. They are known to feed at times on small fishes. In striking into a school of small fish from below they might be led to broach the surface. In towing for plankton food there would be no such occasion. No authentic observation of sockeyes in open ocean has been reported, but inasmuch as no search has been made for them the matter remains without evidence. It is probable that they do not jump in feeding, and thus they are unobserved up to tho time they start for the spawning beds.

FOOD AND FEEDING. THE SOOKEYE.

It is reported that the Fraser River schools, even before leaving Juan de Fuca Strait, have ceased to feed. In Southeast Alaska it was found that a certain percentage of the earlier catches, even at the mouths of the rivers they were presumed to be entering, were still feeding. This is shown in the following table:

Food Ok Adult Sockeyks.

Stomachs of adult sockeyes, as the fish are taken for commercial uses, are commonly empty. In many cases the shrinkage which follows the termination of feeding is pronounced, but usually the upper limb is still lax, with only that degree of contraction due to its emptiness, and the pyloric limb and coeca are still undiminished in size. On the other hand, schools are sometimes taken in which the shrinkage of all parts of the digestive tract is pronounced and the characteristic yellow slimy or curdy secretion fills the canal. The stomachs not infrequently contain scales, teeth, bits of vegetable debris, etc., all of which is probably incident to the pursing of large numbers in the nets and consequent struggles of the fish. In many cases the esophageal cavity is filled with a clear viscid liquid, which appears to be largely dissolved jellyfish.

In the examples examined at Yes Bay in 1905, undissolved portions of the common globular ctenophore frequently occurred. This same form was taken in great abundance in the surface and subsurface towings in the bay and in Behm Canal just off the bay. In addition, fragments were found of what seemed to be the larger ellipsoidal, purple ctenophore taken in towings in Behm Canal and elsewhere only in depths of 50 fathoms or more. It is not known whether this form rises at night, hence its presence indicates nothing as to the depth at which the salmon feeds. Much the greater part of the food observed is crustacean. In the examples from Boca de Quadra, 1903, which have the highest percentage (36.8) of food-containing individuals of any lot examined, the material is almost wholly larval crabs, a few of the macruran forms also occurring. In Kegan examples the common crustacean form is a small macruran, though a few crab larva? also were noted. In Yes Bay the most widely distributed form is a macruran, but crab larva? are present in great quantity. Yes Bay salmon stomachs showed much the same aggregation of forms that the tow net developed, which indicates that the food is taken by "towing."

Among the stomachs of sockeye salmon taken at Karta Bay, in Moira Sound, and at Hetta, were found some containing sand launces *(Ammodytes alascanus)*, in instances as high as S3 individuals in a single stomach. In these waters large schools of sand launces somewhat more than half grown are numerous during July and August. Schools of young herring occur earlier and during the same period, but in only one instance was a herring found in an adult sockeye stomach. In Yes Bay a small clam worm, identified by Dr. J. Percy Moore as *Callizona angelini* (Kinberg) Apstein, was found in 32 stomachs, or over 4 per cent of those examined. Several of these worms were sometimes found in a single stomach, as if they had been assembled by selective feeding. A very few were noted at Boca de Quadra and at Kegan. These worms were taken only in the sub surface to wings at Yes Bay, but they probably came to the surface in the evening at that season.

It is remarked, in general, that the earlier runs of fish contain a higher percentage of feeding individuals than the later. Much depends also on the locality. At Dolomi practically all the fishing is done in a small bay almost at the river's mouth. It is improbable that the fish enter this bay in great numbers until ready to ascend the stream. Of 511 examples opened August 4 to 11, 1904, none contained food; many of these stomachs were shrunken, but some were still lax. Of 200 examined August 21 to 23, 1903, none of the first hundred contained food. These fish were of a distinctive type, more or less characteristic, long, slender, and dark in color. Of the second hundred, taken two days later, 9 were feeding on sand launcea and crustaceans. These were brighter fish of a different type— deeper and more resembling the fish of other localities.

The fishing at Nowiskay was done by a single crew, hence ordinarily all or nearly all were taken near the mouth of the river. In 1904, owing to the scarcity of fish, the crew sometimes hauled in the lower end of the arm, which may help to account for the larger number of feeding fish taken that season. This same circumstance has a bearing on the fish examined at Yes Bay in 1905. A greater part of the fishing was done in Behm Canal than in former seasons. The paucity of food material in the bays may sufficiently explain why the salmon do not approach the rivers until about ready to make the ascent.

Digestion in fishes is ordinarily quite rapid, and for this reason we may be sure that food found has been recently ingested; but the fishing crews are out with the daylight, and our knowledge of the distribution of forms at that hour is too limited to permit any conclusions as to the depth at which salmon feed.

The presence of such large percentages of feeding fish might lead to the supposition that the fish were still on the natural feeding grounds and had not yet been made subject to the changed instincts of approaching maturity. This view is somewhat supported by the absence of food as reported in the large schools of the greater rivers at relatively earlier dates. On the other hand may be noted the fact that the Alaskan schools are much smaller, hence the opportunity to feed, if the instinct to do so still remains, is much better. A salmon stomach at any time, if empty for a period, becomes contracted and gives the appearance of being shrunken. This perhaps is due to the lack of blood in the tissues and the action of the contractile fibers. It is noted in migrating fingerlings as well as in adult fish. With the presence of food and excitation of secretion, blood will return to the tissues, the bulk of the ingested mass will stretch 10731—07 5 the fibers, and the feeding appearance will return." It is probable that the sea habitat of salmon will be ultimately disclosed, if at all, by a study of their food and its distribution.

KING SALMON.

In recent years it has been learned that schools of king salmon feed in the channels and bays of Alaska during the winter. In 1903 they were first observed off Naha Bay late in December. Their presence was apparently due to the presence of a large shoal of herring, upon which they were feeding. The stomachs contained only herring, in one case 9 full-sized fish being counted in the stomach of a salmon that was still hungry enough to take the troll. Since the above date a valuable winter fishery for king salmon has been established.6 Previously they had been taken only at the time the herring were approaching their spawning beaches, about April and May, continuing to a greater or less extent throughout the summer in various regions. Their movement apparently depends entirely on that of the herring, which in turn may be supposed to be governed at other times than its spawning season by the abundance of its food; it is well known to be erratic in its appearance. The problems of the food supply of the herring in Alaska have not been considered.

The appearance of the salmon in Monterey Bay in the spring has been taken to be of the same character, i. e., a moving inshore with their food, which here consists of sardines, anchovies, smelts, and other small fishes, squid, and crustacea.c It has been assumed incidentally that these fish are also on their way to the Sacramento to spawn. It does not appear that any careful study of their food, condition of maturity, or even species has been made.

The facility with which the king salmon is taken with a troll, and the consequent interest of anglers, may account for the fuller knowledge of the winter habits of this species. Of the other four species, only one takes a troll, namely, the coho.

THE COHO.

Little is known of the food of the adult coho. Its habit of approaching the rivers late, when almost sexually mature, and running at once into the stream, makes it difficult to study in this regard. The food contents of the immature cohos taken in Puget Sound have not been reported. The adults are known to take the troll readily, which indicates that they feed on small fishes.' Their early exhibition of this

Gutter, Bulletin U. S. Fish Commission, vol. xxn, 1902, p. 126. *b* See footnote *d* below.

cAnnual Report of the Department of Fisheries of Oregon for 1902, p. 69-78.
d " Since 1904 during the winter fishing for king salmon numbers of cohos also have been taken. Up to 1907 only troll lines have been used, but traps have been prepared for use during 1907-8. " (Fassett.) instinct supports the inference, as does also the character of the mouth parts, teeth, and gillrakers. Two examples were seen at Karta Bay the first of August filled with sand launces; another contained a herring. One example, a female, taken at Quadra early in August, was filled with crab larva?, the same material upon which sockeyes were feeding at the time. HUMPBACK AND DOG SALMON.

The humpback is ordinarily not feeding at the time it is taken in the cannery seines. Of a number examined at Karta Bay early in August, some of the males contained crustaceans and in one instance a sand launce; none of the females had food. At this time the males exceeded the females in number in the ratio of 50 to 15. At Kegan early in August a few humpbacks were found containing the macruran from that locality. At Karluk, July 30, they were found to be feeding about equally on sand launces and crustacea.

The dog salmon has not been examined for feeding habits. Like the coho, it approaches the streams late, and as a rule the stomachs are then empty.

RELATION OF FOOD SUPPLY TO NUMBER OF ADULT SALMON.

The abundance of food has a direct relation to the number of adult salmon that may be produced. The propagation of countless myriads of fry can result only in their cannibalism if the supply of other food is lacking. The dependence of the different species of salmon upon other fishes is probably about in the same ratio as their average size. The largest, the king, is largely dependent on the herring, sand launce, cod, etc., for its subsistence, as are, doubtless, also the coho and dog. The two smaller species, humpback and sockeye, are better adapted to live on the more minute life. They are not known to take a troll at any time. Their food is, at least largely, the food of the species which in turn support the king salmon. The interrelation has reached a nice adjustment in nature which, while not understood in detail, is known to exist. The extinction of the herring might lead to increased food supply for the growing sockeye. At the same time it would deprive the dogfish and king salmon of their natural aliment and cause them to become a menace to the otherwise favored species. Only upon complete knowledge of the various elements of animal life can recommendations be safely made regarding more obvious matters. Empirical regulations may be successful, but rational legislation must ultimately rest upon results from the bolting-silk tow nets and the microscope.

AGE OF ADULT SALMON.

The age of the sockeye at maturity is yet not absolutely determined. It is unnecessary to do more than refer to the four-year theory' based on the quadrennial increase in the Fraser River run. There seems to be sufficient reason for believing four years to be the usual term of life for the sockeye and the king salmon, but experiment has pretty conclusively shown that they may mature in less time or may be retarded beyond that term.

It is possible that the humpback reaches maturity in less time. The rapid growth of the young and the biennial occurrence of the species in Puget Sound may be noted in support of this belief. The small size and irregular number in certain localities may be adduced also. A fish of a short growth-period would be more apt to show rapid fluctuation in numbers than a form overlapping a variable series of years.

At Yes Bay in 1903 many very large males occurred, in some cases reaching a weight of 111 pounds. These were already much "humped" and advanced in sex maturity, whereas the main body of fish were still bright. Their occurrence was unusual and the size extraordinary. The fishermen believed them survivors of a previous season. The grilse form has not been noted among the humpbacks or dogs." It has been reported for the coho by Mr. Patching, but not seen by the writer.

SALMON-MARKING EXPERIMENTS. *Methods.*—In an effort to determine the exact age of maturity, fish have been variously marked. As against the results thus obtained it has been asserted that any mutilations can be of no value, since the mutilated part will regenerate. There have been a number of trials of marks. Hubbard, experimenting in the Clackamas River, by removal of the adipose fin is supposed to have determined maturity to arrive in the king salmon at three, four, and five years—mainly at three. Richardson, at Karluk, by removing the dorsal fin in the same manner, arrived at four years as the average age of the sockeye. In August, 1903, 1,600 sockeye fry, reared for the purpose at the Fortmann Hatchery from the 1902 eggs, were marked by excising both ventrals with fine curved scissors. The fry were released at a point in the Naha just above Heckman Lake as soon as marked, at which time they were about 3 months old. In 1906 between 50 and 100 adult sockeyes with ventral fins missing were reported by the superintendent of the hatchery at Yes Lake from the spawning beds there. Some had also the adipose fin removed; this mark in addition had been used on some of the fry mentioned above. At the Fort mann Hatchery, where they were marked, only 2 of these fish were obtained in 1906." There is no doubt that these fish noted at the hatcheries were identical with the fry so marked. In careful measurements of over 7,000 sockeyes during two summers and casual inspection of many thousands during five seasons in Alaska, the writer has seen but one example of a salmon without ventrals, and in that case the fish was entirely without any indication that fins had ever begun to develop and was doubtless a monstrosity. The 2 samples sent in from Loring show the stubs of the fins just as would be expected from an amputation performed in the manner stated. This experiment, so far, supports the four-year theory.

In the spring of 1904 several thousand of the yearlings trapped at the head of Naha Bay were marked by the complete amputation of both dorsals. These fish were the same age as the fry mentioned above as marked the previous summer. There has been no record of the return of any of these latter. It is believed that the handling resulted in great loss and the percentage of survivors was too small to obtain notice even if, as is probable, the complete regeneration of the fin did not make the marking useless. A similar experiment at the Clackamas hatchery in the summer of 1904 has so far produced no result.

Mr. Rutter made several experiments in branding fingerlings, and reached the conclusion that it can be successfully done. TJnfamiliarity *with,* methods ordinarily used in branding led him first to try a five-pointed star. As was to be expected, when the fish survived the severe burn of the iron, which was seldom, the scar rapidly became formless by obliteration of the points. Subsequent experiments developed that a wire is a better instrument, the heat being applied wholly on fine lines, burning the skin but not injuring adjoining tissue. Any design with lines which do not cross, and which will not resemble in sharp angles or parallels the wounds of the teeth of predatory animals, will answer.

It is believed that if fin amputation is demonstrated as a feasible mark it should be performed on the small fingerlings. Fish under 2 inches are less susceptible to injury by handling. The fingerlings, after the formation of scales, are very easily injured, the scales parting from the skin upon the least touch. Their struggles when handled will almost infallibly produce abrasions. The experiment of anaesthetizing has not been made.

Regeneration of lost parts.—Regarding reproduction of lost parts, authorities differ. It was believed by Giinther 6 that "the power of reproduction of lost parts in Teleosteous fishes is limited to the delicate terminations of the fin rays," etc.

"Seven more of these marked fish have been reported taken at the Fortmann Hatchery during the fall of 1907 up to September 29. b Giinther, Introduction to the study of fishes, p. 188.

Jordan" reiterates essentially the same statement, and this belief was held also by Weismann. Thomas Hunt Morgan has by experiment demonstrated a slightly greater power of regeneration of lost extremities of fins than had previously been held to exist. After amputation of the distal portions of the caudal in the mudfish *(Fundulus heteroclitus)* regeneration was distinctly marked in from seven to twelve days, indicating the ultimate reproduction of a perfect fin. In further experiments both the paired and median fins of this fish were found to possess the power of reproducing the distal portions after amputation. Similar regeneration in the caudal was demonstrated in the common scup *(Stenotomus chrysops)* and the mackerel shad *(Decapterus macarellus).* The presence of this fin-regenerative potency was also noted in the kingfish *(Menticirrhus saxaiilis(1)*), the goldfish *(Oarassius auratus),* a minnow (probably a *Leucisms),* the stone cat *(Notunts* sp.), and others. In a spiny-rayed labroid *(Ctenolabrus)* a pectoral fin cut off *at the middle* regenerated completely, and a pelvic (ventral) fin had partially regenerated when the fish was killed. In the toadfish *(Opsanus tan)* the pectoral fins regenerated only very slowly. In none of these experiments is it stated that a fin was cut away closely at its base. There seems to be no evidence that Gunther's original statement is incorrect. It was shown that in ordinary temperatures the beginning of regeneration is almost immediate where it does occur; hence it is perfectly safe to assume that in the removal of the adipose dorsal in the salmon no regeneration occurs, since no beginning of a new growth is evident several months after its excision. Nor do these experiments militate against the results of the Loring experiment of entire amputation of the ventrals, cited above. It is probable that in very cold water the beginning of regeneration will be much delayed.

SALMON IN THE TROCADERO, AT PARIS.

The most unassailable evidence of the age of king salmon adults has been rendered by the aquarium of the Trocadero[b], in France. At that institution king salmon from eggs obtained in California have been reared for some twenty-five years, generation after generation. It has been found that four years is the usual age, but that females may mature in three and in some cases not until five years. The males are found to be more precocious, some maturing in their second year. This precocity is noted in nature in the "grilse" of the Sacramento and the "Arctic salmon" of the Alaskan sockeye. The occurrence of abnormally large fishes may be due to the delay of maturity until the fifth year. It was found at the aquarium that fish invariably died soon after completion of spawning.

"Jordan, Guide to the study of fishes, vol. I, p. 150.

[b] Bulletin de la Society Nationale d'Acclimatation de France, October, 1905.

The New Zealand experiment in acclimatizing salmon indicates that both the sockeye and the king reach maturity at the age of 4 years. These two species have been successfully transplanted to New Zealand waters, and runs of mature well-developed fish returned in 1906 to the respective streams in which they were placed. An account of the results will appear in the Proceedings of the American Fisheries Society for 1907.

FACTORS INFLUENCING RETURN TO FRESH WATER.

SEX INSTINCTS VERSUS CONDITION OF NUTRITION.

The stimulus which it is assumed impels the salmon to seek again the fresh water is approaching maturity. Many known facts bring this assumption into question. The study of the Atlantic salmon by the Fishery Board for Scotland led to the conclusion that in that species the state of nutrition is the factor determining migration toward the river; that when the fish has accumulated the necessary supply of material it tends to return to its original habitat. In this conclusion it is assumed that the present sea-running race has been derived from a permanent freshwater-residing form. On the other hand it has been assumed for the Pacific salmon that at the time of separation of the early run to begin its travel into the stream, all of that school of salmon—both those that are to leave the sea at once and cease to feed and those that are to remain and continue to feed— are equally well nourished and equally developed. It is known that heavy floods in the springtime bring heavy spring runs, and correspondingly poor fall runs, and it will be shown that the early arrivals in Alaskan short streams are not so heavy in proportion to length as late arrivals. In all salmon the cessation of feeding upon or just previous to entering the fresh water brings a peculiar factor into the problem. When they start for the spawning beds the fish have two demands upon their supply of energy-producing stores, i. e., energy for the work of ascending the rivers, and material for the growth and development of the sex product—spawn and milt. In the case of fish entering long rivers, such as the Columbia and Fraser, the early run enters with a slightly developed generative product to build up and the entire trip to the headwaters to perform. The late run arrives with more fully developed sex organs and a much shorter journey to make.

Since no fish known to enter the streams fail to become sexually mature the same season, and since fish retained permanently in fresh water do not mature the sex product until they have reached the appropriate age, it must still remain as the most reasonable con » See Rutter, Bulletin U. S. Fish Commission, vol. xxn, 1902, p. 109. This can not be cited as an exception to the above statement, since the assumption that the precocious maturation is *due to* residence in fresh water has no other support, and, moreover, sea-run males are known to return as sexually mature grilse.

elusion that the reproductive purpose is mainly instrumental in bringing them into the streams. Correlated with this in determining the particular time of year for the entrance into fresh water are seasonal influences, temperature, density, currents, character of the river, etc. There may be sufficient explanation of the variation in time of runs in the proposition advanced by Moser, viz, that in streams where the run is large both the precocious arrivals and the stragglers are in sufficient number to be noted and recorded. But this can scarcely account for the distinctly double maxima noted in the runs of the Columbia and Sacramento rivers. The sockeye is said to "run" earliest in the Aleutian Islands, where it arrives in May. It is said to be found in the vicinity of Umnak Island all the year, in which case it must be feeding. In Bristol Bay the middle of June is given as the time of arrival, but the run is usually small until in July. At Karluk it is earlier, sometimes the first part of June, while in Southeast Alaska the arrival is delayed in certain streams until the second week in July.

THE DIFFERENT RUNS.

In large rivers different runs of salmon are noted—for example, in the Columbia and Sacramento the king salmon has two runs per year, or two maxima; the early fish are supposed to travel to the headwaters of the various tributaries which they enter, the later run not to ascend so far. The April-June (?) arrivals spawn in July and August; the later fish spawn September to November. The reason for the separation is unknown. A well-marked division appears only in the Columbia and Sacramento. In the former river both king and sockeye are so separated. The Karluk is said similarly to have two runs, one maximum about the last of June and one the first of August, but this was not true in 1903 when the river was under study. A double run might be supposed to bear some relation to the two migration periods of young, i. e., as fry or yearlings, but this is not borne out by the conditions in the Fraser, where such migrations are also known. In the Sacramento, the distance being short and the winters mild, the hatching periods and time of reaching salt water are distinct for each run. In the Columbia the elevation of the headwaters, with attendant low temperatures and distance which the fry must travel to reach the sea, may equalize the time of arrival at salt water.

The question whether an early hatched fry, the offspring of an early run parent, will in turn become an early run adult is of much importance in fish-cultural problems. In the Sacramento both runs receive attention at the propagating stations. On the Columbia it is mainly the late fish that are propagated, with what seems to be the result that early fish are becoming fewer. In the Fraser the early run may escape by reason of the close seasons. In short Alaskan streams both early and late fish occupy the same grounds. The late comers thus destroy the early eggs to a considerable extent. Partly from this cause, perhaps, double runs are not well established; perhaps the fact that the volume of the streams is insufficient to carry the stimulus of the fresh water to the spring feeding ground permits the fish to remain together until all are induced by approaching maturity to direct their movement toward the coast.

Rutter found that of over 25,000,000 artificially hatched fry placed in the Sacramento in 1897-98, in addition to the product of natural reproduction, less than 1,000,000 remained as summer residents. The following year the stations hatched about 17,000,000 from the two runs, with probably a greater natural production than the previous year. The fry passed the lower river between the middle of January and last of March, with maxima about six weeks separated (January 25-30 and March 8-13), or less than half the interval that separates the adult runs, if we assume that the fry taken in January at Walnut Grove were from the early run eggs, as we must by consideration of temperatures and the observed rate of travel. This does not bear out the opinion that runs remain distinct.

TEMPERATURE.

Adjacent streams may have different seasons, i. e., time of run. The variations in the small streams of the Loring district are of interest. The early streams are the Naha, with dates of June 14-26 for the first fishing; Karta Bay, June 13-26, and with these may be included Klawak, June 16-29. The late streams are Yes Bay, July 11-17; the Moira Sound group (Dolomi, Kegan, and Nowiskay), July 8-25; Quadra, July 13. The streams here listed as early streams all drain lake areas of considerable surface and of a character that would occasion an early rise in temperature. The late streams have lakes of smaller total area or greater elevation and high surrounding ridges. The temperature data at hand are entirely too scant to demonstrate the difference suggested, but the few figures obtained seem to point to such a condition. They indicate that the streams are somewhat warmer than the surface in the adjacent salt water at the time of the run, i. e., that the fish leave the colder for warmer water.

June 30 a line of observations was carried from the Naha to Karta Bay. Off Loring the surface was 57, density 1. 0133. With some variations the temperature reached its maximum, 59.5, about midway across Behm Canal, with density lowered to 1.0112; from this point both temperature and density decreased until off Cape Caamano, where the temperature had reached 54.5 and the density had fallen to 1.0108-1.0110. Off the cape a momentary rise in density— 1. 0136—occurred. Crossing Clarence Strait the temperature varied around 55—density rising from 1.012 to 1. 0216—with which increased density the temperature fell again to 51, and this, falling in places to 50, was carried with a density of about 1.020 through Kasaan Bay into Karta Bay, when the density abruptly dropped to about 1.012, with almost no change in temperature.

These figures show a general decrease in temperature corresponding to a rise in density. They show further that the surface density and temperature of Kasaan Bay is little affected by the fresh water from the Karta stream, whereas Behm Canal is markedly affected by its affluents. At this season sockeyes are running into both the colder waters of Karta Bay and the warmer waters of Naha Bay. The Karta Bay fish are reported to be seen first farther south along the west side of Clarence Strait. Hence they may never come in contact with the currents from Behm Canal.

Another series of observations was made July 30 and 31, 1903, from Kegan stream to Dolomi via Old Johnson Stream opposite Kegan. In the Kegan Basin the temperature was 60 and density 1.003; at the Kegan fish scow, anchored just outside the mouth of the stream, the temperature was about 53 and density somewhat over 1.020; in the middle of Moira Sound, between the two streams, the temperature fell to 51 and density rose to near 1.022. In Old Johnson Bay a temperature of 54 and a density of over 1.020 were found. Passing down the sound, the temperature fell gradually, but varying, to 51, with corresponding rise in density to near 1.022. The inflow from North Arm (Nowiskay) could scarcely be noted. The lowest temperature was found off Point Adams, 48, with a density of over 1.022. The stream at Dolomi exhibited no influence outside the arm into which it flows. At the fish scow in the inner bay the temperature was 57 and density 1.0032. Five minutes' run of the tug reached water of 52 F. and density of over 1.020.

If the fish travel on the flood tide, it must be necessary for them to approach these small streams very closely in order to feel the influence. The observations recorded above are all surface, where the greatest change would be made by the fresh water. It would seem scarcely possible to detect the river water outside the small basins or estuaries at a few feet below the surface.

It is not impossible that the incoming schools closely follow the coast line. For example, it has been stated" that sockeyes enter Uyak Bay, on the east side of Harvester Island, pass to the south and east side of the bay, thence to the mouth of Larsen Bay, after which they follow the west side of the bay at some distance from the shore and pass out again into Shelikof Strait at the point where first seen. Since Uyak Bay contains no sockeye streams, such A. B. Alexander, 1ns. notes.

movements of a school, if they occur, can be regarded only as exploration either for food or spawning streams.

Other interesting temperature questions are raised by the sockeyes' selection for spawning of such streams as the one at Bartlett Bay. It may be postulated that streams with lakes at levels accessible to salmon possess a higher summer temperature than streams of similar volume without lakes. There is a class of streams, however, such as that at Bartlett Bay, where the lake outlet furnishes only a small part of the volume of the main stream. In the Bartlett Bay stream a temperature of 46 at the mouth June 26 decreased to 39 before the lake in which the sockeyes spawn was reached. The main volume of the stream is glacial water, and there is nothing at the mouth to intimate to human intelligence the existence of lakes and suitable spawning beds in its course. With even this temperature, however, the river was probably warmer than the surrounding salt water, in which ice was then drifting.

CURRENTS.

The influence of tide or current in salt water apparently varies, for reports are contradictory. The Fraser River sockeyes are said to travel on the flood, i. e., with the current. Salmon enter San Francisco Bay on the ebb. At Karluk they come in on the first of the ebb, or preferably on flood just before the current from the lagoon changes. In the Kvichak the last of the flood and the whole of the ebb are said to be the best fishing. By this they must approach on the flood and take the river on the ebb. It is also claimed that a southwest wind blows the fish inshore in Bristol Bay, whereas a northeast wind at Karluk is alleged to prevent their approach. The value of these observations regarding winds is lessened by the fact that certain winds prevent the operation of gear and perhaps influence the salmon not to expose their presence by jumping. It is believed that many fish, in 1903 estimated at some 2,000,000, reached Karluk Lake in this way by passing the bay and estuary unobserved. A similar instance was noted by Mr. Cobb on the Ugaguk in 1906, when an offshore wind had not prevented the schools from reaching the fishing ground. It seems probable that inshore winds, besides obscuring the presence of fish, will accelerate their movement by assisting the current shoreward, while an opposite wind will retard this.

In such streams as Dolomi it is inconceivable that a current influence can be felt beyond the small bay at its mouth. This may explain why only small fishes reach it, such small fishes perhaps traveling closer to the shore. On the other hand, none of the small salmon streams of that region can maintain the identity of their currents oMoser, Bulletin U. S. Fish Commission, vol. xxi, 1901, p. 374.

far beyond the receiving bays, and if currents are a prominent factor fish entering Behm Canal should all travel to the Unuk.

The influence of flood water on schools near a river's mouth may be due in part to an increased temperature of the water as well as to an augmented volume. It is well known that in dry seasons, when the streams are low, even though a sufficient depth for a practicable ascent may remain, schools tarry in the bays much longer than in rainy seasons. But as this is marked only in the case of small streams, the main factor must be the volume or quantity of water.

ASCENT OF STREAMS.

The speed of the salmons' ascent of rivers is perhaps modified by various conditions. In short streams of Southeast Alaska large fish are not noted in the rivers except while passing difficult falls. In the Naha they seem to make the distance from tide water to the' lakes traveling at night, hence not observed. At Dorr Falls, on the Naha, humpbacks which were constantly jumping at the fall throughout the day made no attempts at night. This lack of movement at night can not hold for waters of other character.

Observations on the Karluk indicated that about ten days were consumed in making the ascent there, a rate of 2 to 3 miles per day, the main movement occurring after 4 o'clock p. m.

Rutter estimated that the spring run of king salmon in the Sacramento ascend from the ocean to their spawning beds at the average rate of 10 miles per day. If some of this time is lost in the ebb and flow of tides in the bay, the rate in the river is in excess of this. The fall run, he determined, ascended the river at the rate of 4 or 5 miles per day. Earlier observers supposed the fall fish to travel the faster." Sockeyes are reported to reach the Quesnel Dam, 500 miles up the Fraser, about the middle of August; in 1906 the first arrived July 26. These are perhaps the fish entering the river in May and June, and if so they travel at a rate between 5 and 10 miles per day up a rapid river—ascending in that time to an altitude of 2,250 feet. The run continues at this point until September, perhaps including a part of the heavy July run at the mouth of the river. This would indicate that the rate of ascent is more nearly the higher figure, or that it is about equal to that of the early Sacramento fish. The variation between this movement and that in the Karluk is notable. Does it indicate any knowledge on the part of the fish as to the extent of the journey that is to be performed 2

No observations are recorded regarding the movement of the coho or of the steelhead. The coho probably ascends rapidly when traveling for such points as the Wallowa and Baker Lake regions. The time occupied by schools of fish in the brackish water before entering

"Report 'on1nissioners of Fisheries, California, 1870-77, p. 10.

the stream proper seems to vary with locality, species, and time of year. In some cases it is perhaps necessary that some time be so spent to inure the fish to the fresh water. Their natural timidity in approaching shallows has been mentioned above. This may be due to the exposure entailed or to recognized dangers in swift water. Adult sockeyes released at the foot of Seton Lake passed through the 17 or 18 miles of that body of water to its upper extremity in from eight and one-half to about eleven hours, presumably in daylight. INTERVAL BETWEEN ARRIVAL AND SPAWNING.

The early arrivals of salmon spend some time in the region of the spawning beds before depositing any spawn. In the Naha the first sockeyes reach the lakes in June, but none spawn earlier than about the middle of August—after a lake residence of about six weeks. In the Karluk in 1903 the first sockeyes entered the lake about the middle of June; they continued to arrive in numbers until the latter part of July. They spawned during August. The first arrivals, as in the Naha, thus spent about six weeks in the lake and all remained at least four weeks before spawning. In the Fraser basin in 1905 the first fish reached Seton Lake the latter part of July, the run continuing until the latter part of September. The first eggs were spawned the first week of September, and spawning continued until late in October. This was approximately the same length of residence before spawning as in the Naha and the Karluk.

During the residence in the lakes it is improbable that the fish occupy the greater depths, since it has been shown that these are not suitable for fish life. In the evenings salmon may often be seen in numbers "finning," i. e., swimming leisurely at the surface in such manner as to expose the dorsal fin. The sockeye seldom jumps in lakes until about to approach the spawning bed, when there may be a slight demonstration of that habit. Ordinarily a lake may be filled with adult fish and no evidence of their presence noted by the observer.

The early king salmon also reach the beds some time before spawning. They reach the McCloud late in June or early in July, but do not spawn until the middle of August. In the Idaho investigation it was found that they reached the upper Salmon Valley the last half of July, the spawning occurring approximately a month later. All sockeyes had entered Alturas Lake before July 20 and spawned from the 23d until into September, the height of the season being about the last of August. The fish seem to have spent at least a month in the lake.

The late-running species—coho, humpback, and dog—arrive only a short time before maturity.

PARENT STREAMS.

The election by salmon of certain streams as a spawning ground to the exclusion of others has long been noted in the case of the sockeye and king salmon. The choice on the part of the latter seems to be based mainly on the volume, only stragglers of this species entering the smaller streams like the Naha and Yes rivers. The larger streams, such as the Stikine and Unuk, carry large quantities of silt and thereby form extensive mud flats, which, with the drift carried on the strong currents, make fishing difficult. For this reason no adequate idea of the number of king salmon entering these streams has been obtained. The only small stream in the region near Loring which they are known to frequent, one tributary to Carroll Inlet, has not been examined. They are commonly thought to have in Alaska a predilection for streams of glacial origin, but all large rivers of this section have some glacial water.

The sockeye is recognized as exclusively a frequenter of streams with tributary lakes. The only suggestion adverse to this is a report by Mr. Fred Patching, superintendent of the Fortmann Hatchery, regarding a small stream in the vicinity of Wrangell, which Mr. Patching believes to have no lake water. The sockeyes are said to spawn in a somewhat expanded portion of the stream, but this expanse has not the character of a lake. As a converse proposition, not all lake outlets, even of apparently suitable character, attract the sockeye. The Anan stream, tributary to Bradfield Canal, seems to be perfectly adapted to all the sockeye's requirements, but no recognized run enters it.

The dog salmon apparently recognizes some distinctions, though it is much more generally distributed than the two above-mentioned species. For example, comparatively few of this cpecies enter the Naha or Yes rivers, whereas Karta River, on the opposite side of the strait, abounds with it.

The coho is probably less particular in its requirements. The fry were found, without exception, in every stream and brook examined; even a tiny seepage rill entering Naha Bar which would become dry with the first week of fair summer weather contained its little school of coho fry. That some streams are profitably fished for cohos, whereas others apparently as suitable are found not productive, is probably due mainly to the stream character, this in the one case being such as to promote the schooling of the fish at the mouth of the stream, while in the other a greater length of estuary or greater volume permits immediate ascent.

The humpback, like the coho, is found everywhere, and being exceedingly abundant is the more noticeable of the two.

The evidence in the question as to the existence of a homing instinct in the salmon is still lacking in many points. The exposition by H. S. Davis in the Pacific Fisherman (vol. i, no. 6, July, 1903, p. 6 and 7) summarizes the data as known up to that time. The facts advanced as evidence of the existence of such instinct are: (1) Distinctive and characteristic runs in various streams; (2) return of marked salmon to the stream in which liberated; (3) introduction into streams not previously frequented.

"introduction Into Streams Not Previously Frequented."

On this subject little material data beyond Davis's citations is at hand. There is no report that runs have been established in either Papermill Creek or Chinook River. The release of fry in the Chinook River has been continuous since 1898, with no definite result. The presence of salmon in abundance in Tomales Bay has been reported, but seems to be only a result of their general abundance throughout the streams of northern California, and can not be credited to the plants in Papermill Creek. The introduction of Pacific salmon into streams of the eastern United States or of Europe seems not yet to have been successful. Until complete knowledge of the environmental requisites of the different species is obtained, the failure to establish them in these locations can not be accounted for.

The station at Baird, Cal., was opened in 1872 for the collection of salmon eggs for shipment to other streams, mainly in order to introduce the species into the waters of the Atlantic coast. The experiment was conducted on' a scale unprecedented. The first plant was of about 6,000 fingerlings in the Susquehanna at Harrisburg in March, 1873. During the next three years over 640,000 were planted in the Great Lakes system, over 3,250,000 in Atlantic coast streams, over 1,000,000 in tributaries, of the Gulf of Mexico, principally in the Mississippi and its branches, and several hundred thousand were scattered about in the lakes of Minnesota, Colorado, and Utah. To these plants 18,250,000 fry were added in the next five years. The last large plant was made in 1881, at which time the result had become less hopeful and the demand for more attention to the California home waters more urgent. This attempt at acclimatization was based entirely on the fact that the salmon is known to leave the cold ocean water and enter the warm rivers for spawning. The Sacramento rises to a temperature of over 80 and the Columbia reaches almost the same. Conditions appeared to be practically equivalent on the opposite coast, so far as temperature, volume, length, source, and nature of the rivers, the presence of food and enemies, etc., are concerned. But the attempt was an absolute failure.

The success recently attained in introducing both sockeyes and king salmon into the streams of New Zealand should supply valuable data not only on the life history of these species but especially on the physical requisites for practical work. The returning adults in these instances reached only the streams in which the fry had been placed, the two species not commingling. It is yet too early to draw positive conclusions regarding the relative influence of the two factors, natural suitability of the different streams, and a homing instinct.

That any given stream within the natural range of a species is not inhabited would seem to indicate its natural unsuitability. Whether the example of the Chinook River, where the king salmon once placed in the current of the river seems to find the locality at least endurable, can stand as a refutation remains yet to be proved. That it is not naturally populated by this species has been explained by the peculiar nature of its location and the general character of the stream and its bed. At least one of the principal guides directing the salmon to their spawning grounds seems to be the current. That the fish do not enter the Chinook River by choice is thought to be due to the lack of any sensible current from that stream reaching into the path followed by the schools in their movement from the ocean into the Columbia River. Temperatures have not been recorded. This same apparent influence of the current has been noted in many instances. For example, in the Columbia, salmon pass the Willamette during the summer season of flood, when the tributary river has become back water, but enter it before and after that season when the current is perceptible. At the Quesnel Dam in the Fraser system sockeyes died fighting the swift current of the race, while ignoring the feeble flow from the original fishway.

"return Of Marked Salmon."

The experiment in which the marked Naha fry subsequently appeared as adults at Yes Bay, as noted above, must be again mentioned. This result is a direct refutation of the homing theory. The relative numbers at Yes Bay and the Naha are the more remarkable for the reason that no Naha fish are taken except for breeding, hence almost all the individuals returning to that stream would be discovered, while at Yes Bay many may have been taken in the cannery seines and the record lost. In all experiments based on marking young fish by various mutilations the possibility of regeneration of the lost parts must be fully taken into consideration. In this experiment it is believed the fins were cut much closer than in the laboratory experiments.

"distinctive And Characteristic Runs."

Upon this point some more or less conclusive facts have been determined. The group of streams fished by the Loring Cannery were studied in 1903 and 1904, careful counts and measurements of a number of fish from each locality being taken at the receiving scows in order to eliminate as far as possible any doubt regarding the region to which the fish belonged.

The localities are rather widely distributed. The most northerly and most distant from the ocean is Yes Bay, on the upper arm of Behm Canal. Opposite the mouth of this arm, and across Clarence Strait, is Karta Bay at the head of Kasaan Bay. The other localities are near the opening of Clarence Strait into Dixon Entrance; on the west side, Kegan and Nowiskay, tributary to Moira Sound, and Dolomi just above it; on the east side, Boca de Quadra, opening into Revillagigedo Channel; Tamgas, on Annette Island, about midway between Moira Sound and Boca de Quadra, and Port Chester, just above Tamgas, off Nichols Passage.

To make these data of decisive value it remains to be proved that fish taken in the receiving bay of a given stream are all destined, if not interfered with, to enter that stream for spawning. It has been suggested that fish may congregate in a given bay for a time and, subsequently scattering, travel to distant streams to spawn. To test this, Rutter in 1903 tagged several hundred fish and released them in Karluk Bay or in the lagoon. But one of these was ever reported in another basin; most of them were retaken in the seines working in the bay at that time. If not taken the same day, they were seldom found, though occasionally a straggler was discovered several days after its release, the latest nine days after tagging. While not at all definite, these results point to the probability that few, if any, fish reach another river after appearing at the mouth of one. (See also p. 106.)

In some instances, in closely adjacent

basins, the fishermen in their effort to meet the incoming schools reach the neutral grounds between; for example, at Yes Bay some crews fish Behm Canal and so, perhaps, interrupt schools bound for the Unuk River; Moira Sound fishermen sometimes fish outside the respective arms. But this does not often occur. In general, the figures from a given basin are believed to represent fairly well the fish traveling at the time for that particular stream.

Variations in weights and measurements.—In this inquiry weights were taken on a small spring balance read to the nearest quarter pound. The lengths were taken with a steel tape, the fish lying on a flat table. The points chosen, with the view of later making comparative measurements on spawned fish, were the center of the eye and the extremity of the last caudal vertebra. The reading was made to the nearest half centimeter. The depth was taken at the front of the rayed dorsal by means of dividers, which were read from a scale to millimeters. As all the measurements with the exception of the Port Chester and Tamgas figures were made by the writer, the 10731—07 6 personal factor is well guarded against. The exceptions mentioned are measurements made by Fassett after careful observation, and are believed to be closely comparable with the rest. The averages are given in the following table:

Table 2.—Average Weights And Measurements Of Sockeye Salmon From Different Localities.

Of 100 sockeyes, equally divided as to sex, weighed at Karta Bay August 2, 1904, the males averaged 7 pounds and the females 6. Males were very slightly in excess in number at the time.

Differences In Averages Of The Sexes. Except where the mlnus slgn appears, the figures represent excess ln average of the males.

It will be noted that this table shows a smaller average size for the fish-of 1904, except in one instance (Kegan); there the number obtained in 1903 was too small for accurate comparison.

The variation in depth between the two sexes seems to be practically constant, about 1 per cent of the measured length (which measurement is about three-fourths of the total length), or less than 1 per cent of the total length. The dates at which the examinations were made do not alter this ratio, showing that ordinarily there is no great increase of the depth in the male while still in salt water, and that variations of proportionate depth, as shown in the different localities, are not an effect of secondary sex changes. In all instances the males are heavier, although in a few cases slightly shorter than the females. This difference in weight varies from 3.6 per cent in the case of one lot of Quadra fish to over 15 per cent in the case of the Nowiskay fish of 1904. The greater weight is attributable to the greater depth of the males, which exceeds the depth of the females by from 4 to over 7 per cent on the average. In these sex variations there seems to be no marked similarity in the two seasons for a given locality, the resemblance between different localities being greater in some cases than between different years in the same locality. In the few weights of Karta Bay fish taken in August, 1904, the difference in average of the two sexes is remarkable, amounting to over 16 per cent. This is probably due to the increased weight of the later running males. In all questions involving weight, analysis should be made to see what increase is due to mere increase of water in the tissues.

The onty spawned sockeyes weighed were at the Fortmann Hatchery. These were apparently a somewhat different fish from those of other localities, so no data as to the loss suffered during migration and spawning could be deduced. Seventy-two males averaging 539 mm. (std.) in length (480-605) averaged 7.4 pounds in weight, or considerably heavier than fresh fish of the same length from other localities. The combined average of green fish of similar lengths from Yes and Karta bays is but 7.2 pounds. The 128 females measured show an average length (std.) of 532 mm. (465-570) and an average weight of 6 pounds. The combined average of Karta and Yes Bay females of similar length is about 6.3 pounds.

The figures obtained are hardly sufficient to determine the change, if any, incident to the varying periods of the run. Nowiskay is the only locality in which the measurements were carried through a considerable length of time. At this point, owing to the smallness of the early July run, the dates extended from July 14 to 22, and again to August 10, 12, and 31. In summing up these lots as July fish and August fish it is observed that the average length of the July fish is greater. Over 79 per cent of the whole number, 235, measured in July, are over 500 mm. (std.) in length, whereas of the August fish, 277 in number, only 47 per cent exceed 500 mm. The same fact is noticeable in the fish of Karta Bay in 1903. Of 55 measured the first of July nearly 62 per cent arc 550 mm. (std.) or over, whereas of 153 measured the latter part of that month only 45 per cent reach these lengths. These figures pertain only to the males, the females showing less variation. At other stations the daily distribution of sizes very closely resembles the totals, and a curve plotted for any one day would not vary materially from the curve for the total."

The fish of Yes Bay are found to be the heaviest and also the deepest, those of Tamgas the lightest and relatively the most slender. The former are about twice the average weight of the latter, oneeighth longer (total), and one-seventh greater in proportionate depth. These are comparatively widely separated localities; but the variation between more adjacent regions, as Boca de Quadra and Tamgas, while less than in the case of Yes Bay and Tamgas, is still marked. A yet more interesting instance is seen in the streams of Moira Sound and Dolomi.

The average weight of fish from Nowiskay is nearly one-third greater than that of the Dolomi fish, and they are nearly one-sixth longer and of somewhat greater proportionate depth. These basins are immediately adjacent and this difference is always well recognized by the fishermen. It indicates one of three things: That the fish exercise some selective instinct in choosing their spawning stream; that they are practically limited in their feeding activity to a radius of less than 10 miles, or that the currents are such that the product of these two streams remain as separate schools in different areas.

« At. Karluk it is reported (Alexander, ms.) that the earliest-run sockeyes are smallest, averaging Hi to the ease when eanned. As the season advances the size increases until 11 or 11J make a case; but again by the middle or latter part of August'the size falls to about that of the beginning. This may hold in other localities, the earliest of the run passing unobserved by reason of the small number.

In table 3 are shown for the males the percentages in which each weight (to the nearest half pound) was found in the respective lots. In diagram B are plotted the curves for each lot for 1904, the weights being marked off in the horizontal axis and the number of examples of each weight, as a percentage of the whole number weighed at a given locality, indicated on the verticals.

Table 3.—Weights Of Male Sockeyes, Shown As Percentages Of The Total Number Of Examples Exam1ned From Each Local1ty.

In table 4 are shown for the males the various lengths tabulated by percentages of the number of fish in the lots measured, in the same manner as in table 3 to show the weights. In diagram c are plotted the curves for each lot measured in 1904; in diagram D the curves for the lots of 1903 and 1905. Table 4a shows in the same manner the lengths of female sockeyes.

Table 4.—Lengths Op Male Sockeyes, Shown As Percentages Of The Total Number Of Examples Examined 1n Each Local1ty.

Table 4a.—Lengths Of Female Sockeyes, Shown As Percentages Of The Total Number Of Examples Exam1ned For Each Local1ty.

Table 5 shows the depths of the males tabulated in the same manner as the lengths and weights, showing these measurements in percentages of the total number of fish in each lot measured.

Diagram E presents the same information for 1904 shown by curves.

Table 5.—Depths Of Male Sockeyes, Shown As Percentages Op The Total Number Op Examples Exam1ned For Each Local1ty.

A close correspondence will be seen in all the curves for Dolomi and Tamgas." The greatest number of individuals in each are 4-pound fish. The balance of the average weights of the two lots is destroyed by the varying numbers under and over this maximum. The weight curve, however, for Dolomi is very similar to that for Tamgas, though it occupies a place about 0.5 pound higher in the scale, the average weight for Dolomi being 4.5 pounds as compared with 3.9 pounds. An examination of the length curves (diagram E) also shows a very close parallel between these two localities, while the difference between the curves for depths (diagram F) will explain the greater weight of the Dolomi examples, the depth curve for Dolomi standing about 5 mm. higher on the scale than that for Tamgas. Comparing the two lots, it is shown that while the average length is about the same for each locality, and the number of examples of any given length is about the same for each, the Dolomi fish average about 5 mm. greater in depth and therewith 0.5 pound greater in weight. These two localities seem to be set off clearly from all others examined.

"In the following discussion of the tabular data reference is to the male; only unless otherwise specified.

The Dolomi fish of 1903, only 200 in number, were much heavier than those of 1904, but in this they but follow the rule exhibited by other localities, in almost all of which the 1904 fish are lighter than those of the previous year. It will be noted that in 1904 the examination of Dolomi fish preceded that of Tamgas fish by about two weeks. The latter were reported to be quite immature sexually, apparently more so than the Dolomi fish of the earlier date. This may account in a measure for their slenderness. In both these localities running small fish, two type forms are noted more distinctly than in streams carrying the larger fish, viz, the slender terete form, usually dark, with scales more or less embedded, but not showing the other marks of sex maturity; and the deeper, more compressed form, with scales distinct and brightly colored. Fassett noted at Tamgas that one or the other of these forms predominated on different *d &js,* indicating a difference in schools. The dark fish may be fish which have been feeding in the brackish water for some time.

The fish of Karta and Yes bays, the heaviest of all, in 1904 approached one another closely in average weight, varying only 0.3 pound. Examination of the curves for weight, however, shows great difference. The curve for Karta Bay is comparatively simple, rising to over 24 per cent on 7 pounds, extremes falling between 3.5 and 9.5 pounds and showing little tendency to indicate a double node or maximum, while Yes Bay shows 2 maxima, one on 6 pounds and one on 8 pounds, with small numbers on 7 and 7.5; in addition the upper extreme rises to 10.5 pounds. The length curves exhibit this variance increased. In this the line for Karta, showing some tendency to form a double node, rises on the same maxima with Yes Bay, 490 mm. for the lower, and 550 mm. for the upper, but in the case of Yes Bay the percentages on each are about equal (12 per cent), while for Karta they are, respectively, 3 + and 21.5 per cent. This shows that the relatively short fish are found in much greater number among the Yes Bay examples, reducing the total average length (std.) in this locality to 525 mm. as against 538 at Karta, in the face of a slightly higher average weight for Yes Bay. Reference to the depth curve again offers the explanation. The two length types of Yes Bay cause the depth curve for that locality to be somewhat truncated, rising to about equal height (14 to 16 per cent) on 140, 150, 160 mm. and reaching an extreme of 180 mm. This indicates the prevalence of short deep fish in Yes Bay and long slender fish in Karta Bay.

In this year the Karta fish were examined about six weeks earlier than those of Yes Bay. They were noted as nearly all bright, but some were of advanced maturity, with the usual changed form. The Yes Bay fish were noted as being of "advanced" maturity in outward appearance, and it was said they were so from the beginning of the run. The catches made in Behm Canal averaged smaller fish and brighter. The fishermen thought these were "Unuk River fish." Whether regarded as fish traveling to another basin or as a later run not yet ready to enter the bay, these smaller fish account for the abundance of 6-pound fish and the double node in the curve. In 1903 the fish of these two localities, examined at approximately the same time, differed much more in averages, the Yes Bay fish exceeding those of Karta Bay by more than 1 pound in weight, by 12 mm. in length, and about 15 mm. in depth. In neither is there an indication of more than one type. The curves for length, weight, and depth show a single maximum, that for length in both localities on 560 mm., for weight on 7.5 and 8 pounds, respectively, for Karta and Yes bays, and for depth on 145 and 160 mm. Over 25 per cent of the Yes Bay fish reach the maximum, while of the Karta fish less than 20 per cent are of maximum weight and length and 24 per cent are of maximum depth. This indicates, again, that increased weight is largely due to increased depth. In condition the Karta fish of this year were noted as being quite as much, if not more, advanced than the Yes Bay. This applies rather to the last lot of 153, examined July 23 to 26, in which the shorter fish predominated, only 45 per cent being over 550 mm. in length, while of the first lot of 55, examined July 1, 62 per cent were of that length. In the two lots from Yes Bay the curve for that of 1903, taken earliest—about a month earlier than the 1904 lot—is much more like the curves for Karta than like that of Yes Bay for 1904, rising to over 25 per cent on 560 mm., with extremes between 480 and 610. In 1905 the values are more distributed, varying between 10 and 15 per cent from 520 to 570 mm., with extremes between 420 and 590. The average lengths, respectively, of the 1903 and 1905 examples are 555 and 532 mm., the average depths approximating 158 mm. in both cases, while the weights are 8.3 and 8.2 pounds. This indicates that the fish of 1905 were more of the deep form, while those of 1903 were rather long and comparatively slender. These 1903 fish were from the early part of the run, those of 1905 some weeks later, giving another example of the long slender type form in the early run. On the whole, it seems that Yes Bay fish may be said to be deeper than the Karta fish of corresponding maturity, and that the early fish of both localities are of less depth and weight for corresponding length than later fish.

Quadra and the Moira Sound streams, Kegan and Nowiskay, show an almost exactly equal average weight in the fish examined in 1904, as well as close similarity in the averages of length and depth. Inspection of the curves, however, shows this similarity to be factitious. The Quadra fish are a symmetrical group, while the Moira Sound fish are, like Yes Bay, composite, apparently made of a short deep type, and another correspondingly longer and more slender.

The branchiostegal rays exhibit little local variation in number. The maximum in practically all cases falls on 14/13, the left overlapping membrane carrying the extra ray; about one-third the total occurs on this maximum. Extremes are 12/11 and 16/15. Quadra and Kegan resemble one another in rising high on 13/13 and failing low on 14/14 and the higher counts. Karta and Dolomi exhibit the highest counts on 14/14. In no instance was a clearly defined case of right overlapping seen, though occasionally the right membrane carries the higher number of rays.

Table 8.—Branch1osteoal Ray Count.

In the number of tubes in the lateral line (table 9) no great local riation was found, the averages varying from 132.1 to 135, with tremes 126 and 143. The value of this count is somewhat lessened T the varying degree to which the tubes extend on the caudal, tiis does not imply that all the high counts are due to this; in some stances high counts are due to the finer scaling. In other cases ren low counts continued well on to caudal. The averages for the ifTerent years, however, show a striking similarity. The maxima ary from 132 for Karta in 1904 to 135 for Dolomi in 1903, but lostly fall on 133.

Table 9.—Tubes Ok Lateral Line.

In table 10, showing rows of scales, it will be seen that the counts for 1903 regularly fall below those for 1904. This is due to the varying procedure regarding the fine rows in front of dorsal and ventral fins, where the counts were initiated. A considerable variance is thus introduced. The branching of the rows under the front of the dorsal also affected the accuracy of the count. In some specimens a few scales' difference in the point at which this branching occurs adds or excludes a row in the count, which was made for the top rows from front of rayed dorsal down to lateral line, and for lower rows from front of ventrals up to lateral line, the lateral row being included in the total.

Table 10.—Rows Op Scales.

The average number of rows of scales varies from 43 to nearly 46, with extremes 38 and 52. It was noted that the slender type form usually showed a slightly smaller number of rows.

In conclusion, it may be stated that the various counts, while not amounting to demonstration, point to similarity in fishes from a given basin rather than to a heterogeneous mixture of schools. In general the environment at any one locality is very like that at any other; hence if the output of each stream were entirely segregated there would scarcely arise great differences of character among the different lots. The range of variation is, in fact, so small that it appears to fall within the possible effect of the personal factor if the counts were made by different individuals; or of changing schools in any given stream if made by the same individual in sequence. With measurements, however, there is a difference. A sufficient number of fish for the purpose can be measured in a few days spent at any one locality, and the time element may be controlled by frequent change of place and renewed examinations at each. The remarkable difference found between the fish of such adjacent localities as Dolomi and the Moira Sound streams clearly proves the value of such data."

STREAMS NOT UTILIZED BY SOCKEYES.

It is unfortunate in the study of Alaska salmon that almost no streams not known to be frequented by sockeyes have been examined. The only exception of importance is the Anan of Bradfield Canal, which was visited on August 31, 1905. This stream is noted as the earliest and most productive humpback stream in Southeast Alaska. It is slightly less than the Naha in volume and about 3 miles in length below the first lake. Nowhere in the course are any impediments to salmon at ordinary stages of water. The lake has about 160 feet of elevation, and on the above date had a surface temperature of 59.5, about 1 degree higher than the stream. A tributary of the stream was 54. At that time humpback and king salmon in small numbers were seen, and there were a few scattering red fish which were thought to be sockeyes. Two humpbacks were seen to jump in the lake. There is no apparent reason why sockeyes should not ascend this stream in numbers equal to the runs in such streams as those of Moira Sound. An examination of the lake might reveal some obstacle to their natural propagation. There was nothing at that season apparent in the surface densities or temperatures to deflect a run entering Clarence Strait. From this strait through Ernest Sound and into Bradfield Canal the temperatures were in general increasing, 54 to 58, and densities decreasing, 1.020 to about 1.010. In Beh. m a For a similar study of the winter flatfish *(Plcuroneetcs americanus)*, see Hermon C. Bumpus, On the identification of fish artificially hatched. American Naturalist, vol. XxxI1, June, 1898, p. 407-412.

Canal at the same time temperatures rose from 55 at the head of Tongass Narrows to 58 off Spacious Bay, densities falling from 1.0188 to 1.0124 at the same time. Subsurface tows demonstrated an abundance of plankton food throughout all the channels.

Ketchikan Creek is a larger stream than Helm Bay Creek, which carries a few thousand sockeyes. It drains a lake and is frequented by humpbacks and cohos. No sockeyes are known to enter it. They could not reach the lake owing to falls about a mile from the mouth, but a school of fish looking for a suitable stream would learn this fact only after ascending the river.

A few hundred yards below its head Naha Bay receives a small creek known as Steelhead Creek. This creek drains lakes of considerable size, and should carry water suitable for sockeyes, though they could not enter the lakes on account of an intercepting fall. The volume is small, but during the rainy season is ample for the ascent of fish, and many coho, dog, and humpback salmon, as well as steelheads, spawn there. No sockeyes are known to enter it, nor were any sockeye fry seen among the thousands of salmon fry taken there.

It is probable that examination of the unstocked streams of Alaska would disclose others of interest in the question of stream selection.

RELATION OF SIZE OF RUN TO SPAWNING AREA.

There seems to be no relation between the size of the run at any given stream and the extent of spawning ground. Hetta, considered good for from 50,000 to 150,000 fish, has comparatively little area of beds. The fish spawn mainly in one small creek about a mile in length, and along the lake shores. The Naha, as noted above, has a small area compared to its natural productiveness. Kegan has almost no spawning bed—only about a hundred yards of the main stream. At Nowiskay the borders of the lake are used almost entirely, none of the entering streams being suitable. Yes Bay and Karta streams both have excellent and extensive beds. On the other hand, the stream at Ward Cove has a greater area of good spawning ground than any of these streams except Karta and Yes bays, yet it yields too few sockeyes to pay for fishing. Karluk Lake has many tributary creeks that are used by spawning fish, but the total area seems scarcely commensurate with the enormous productiveness.

With the exception of the few streams just mentioned, little is known of the spawning grounds of the Alaskan sockeye. Up to 1903 no attempt was made to arrive at the natural fecundity of the spawning beds; hence the investigator is absolutely without standard or means of accurate comparison.

SELECTION OF SPAWNING GROUND. CONDITIONS REQUIRED BY THE SOCKEYE.

Interesting preferences are shown by the mature salmon on coming out of the lakes to spawn. The first run of sockeyes at Fortmann Hatchery (usually of somewhat smaller fish) enters McCune Creek. This creek is a mile or so in length and drains a slope to the southeastward of the lake, the mouth, as will be seen from the map, being but a few yards from the entrance of the main stream. The lower course is over fine gravel and has but a moderate fall.

On July 28, 1903, Heckman Lake at the surface was 64, Naha River at the hatchery 60, McCune Creek 53. There were no spawners in sight. August 27 the river was 61 and the creek 52$, and fish had been spawning a week. At this time some fish were showing a preference for the creek, which was fenced. Considerable numbers of ripe fish were in the river. October 15 the river was about 46; November 17, 36.

Selective discrimination is also shown in Jordan Lake. Emma Creek, tributary to that lake, has a small lake near its source in which its water is somewhat warmed. Gibson Creek, a larger stream, evidently has no expansion in its course, for its waters are always cold. Sockeyes are never known to spawn in Gibson Creek, which carries a temperature of 48 or less, while Emma Creek, between 50 and 60, is to a small extent made use of.

August 18, at Nowiskay, North Arm of Moira Sound, the main stream above was 51, the lake over the spawning beds 62$. A few fish were in sight, but none spawning. This stream is 44 and the lake 46 to 45 during the spawning season. No sockeyes enter the stream, though dog and humpback salmon do. The sockeyes spawn about the lake shores.

At Karta Lake, September 11, Willow Creek was 50§; Alder Creek, 47 $. Sockeyes were spawning in both in about equal numbers, or slightly preferring Willow Creek, perhaps for its greater size. The main river below the lake was 53$ and full of dog and humpback salmon.

At Yes Bay, September 19, 1903, the river above was full of spawning sockeyes, temperature 50; sockeyes were also entering the flooded creeks at 70. September 14, 1904, the surface of the lake was 52, the water over the beds, 49. 5; in the pool above, 48.5; a feeder of this pool, 46. May 2, 1905, the temperature of the main stream had reached 49. Early in September of that year salmon were spawning in water of 51.

At Quadra, August 1, 1903, the lake surface was 63 to 65. Osten Creek, at the head of the lake, in which the fish spawn, 51 at 3 p.m.; the sockeyes had just begun to appear at this stream. A fine creek farther down the lake was 57; it is said few sockeyes enter this. The hatchery brook was 46. The bay just off the stream August 5 was 64 at 6 p. m. , or practically the same as the outflow from the lake.

At Kegan, October 3, fish were spawning in the main stream above at 47 and refusing a smaller stream at 43 flowing through the same mouth; later they were reported to be spawning in both, temperatures unknown, but doubtless equalized to a degree.

At Ward Cove, September 6, a few sockeyes were spawning in the stream at 55, but this is not a sockeye stream, properly speaking, though it has the required lake and an extensive stretch of good spawning bed.

In the Wallowa Dr. Kendall observed that the dwarf sockeye preferred the warmer water after temperatures fell below 45, though spawning continued until the temperature had dropped to 40.

These observations indicate that the natural spawning temperature for the sockeye is between 47 and 55, probably not over 50 by preference. (See p. 97.) The natural fall temperature for creeks not draining lakes or extensive swamps is about 45 to 48, lake outlets 55 to 60. The presence in a stream's course of a lake of any large size and a low altitude may usually be at once discovered by temperature, except, of course, when the lake outflow is mingled with another stream of low temperature, as from a glacier. Ordinary springs have a summer temperature of 44 to 48, winter around 40. Creeks, of course, fall with the air temperature to freezing.

In the same manner in which they approach the ascent of a river from the sea, the sockeyes school about the spawning stream a short time before entering, and after entering the current proceed by easy stages to the bed finally occupied. Frequently they are seen to drift back over a riffle they had almost surmounted, and appear in most cases to enter swift water with hesitation and caution. It was noted at the Fortmann Hatchery when high water prevented the usual seining of ripe fish that the natural spawning did not commence for a day or so after the fish covered the beds. A short time seems to be spent in selecting nests.

The sexes of the Alaska sockeyes as found during the fishing season are approximately equal, or perhaps there is more commonly a slight excess of males. Of 1,025 examined at Karta Bay June 24 to July 8, 1904, the sexes were equal; 548 of the first arrivals at Nowiskay July 14-22 had an excess of 12 males, while of 551 at this same place August 10-31 males were still in excess by 19. At Kegan from July 24-29, 988 examples showed 28 in favor of the females; Yes Bay July 26-28, 1905, had an excess of males by 10 in 510, while on August 14 among 172 fish the females exceeded by 24; August 16-20, 1904, in 976 examples there were 31 more males 10731—07 7 than females. Dolomi August 4-11 showed a surplus of 21 males in 990; at Quadra August 24-29, 967 examples had an excess of 45 males. These figures show an average preponderance of males by 1.3 per cent. There seems to be no difference in the time of arrival of the two sexes. One sex may be more numerous on one day's fishing and the other on the following day.

It is stated that in the Fraser during the first of the run, the males are greatly hi excess. The presence of unmated males is to a certain extent damaging, since they go through the spawning movements alone, and thus disturb the beds. Under wholly natural conditions there should be practical equality in numbers of the two sexes.

PREFERENCES OF THE KIXG SALMON.

The king salmon spawns in higher temperatures than the sockeye. On the McCloud River it begins spawning at a temperature of about 56, the summer run completing the season within 3 or 4 of that temperature. In Battle Creek the fall run spawns in practically the same range. That they habitually seek a less depressed temperature than the sockeye is shown by their spawning below the lakes into or beyond which the latter species invariably continues. This has been noted at Karluk, on the Wallowa, and on the Salmon and Payette rivers in Idaho, though in short streams like the Yes Bay Stream the straggling king salmon may also go above the first lake. But while this temperature is suitable a higher can not be endured. It has been found that the summer run can not be successfully confined in lower Battle Creek. These fish naturally travel to the cooler upper reaches, and retention in the warmer water of the lower course causes their death.

At the Trocadero Aquarium it was found that fish of 3 and 4 years can not endure a summer and fall temperature of more than 61; an addition of 3 or 4 degrees is fatal. Moreover, at that period an abundance of water is essential. This latter condition, perhaps, enables the fish safely to make the ascent of the heated waters of the Sacramento. During May, when the height of the summer run is passing, the river temperatures range closely about 60, at which temperature the fish are able to move at the rate of 10 miles per day. In August, when the fall run is traveling up the river, the temperatures are decreasing from about 80 to 74. At this temperature they travel but half as fast, though at a more advanced stage of maturity. During October and November the temperatures continue to fall, varying at Sacramento City from 70 to 60, and 60 to 50 during the respective months. At this time the spawning temperatures of 50 to 55 are found in the middle course of the river, and in seasons when the depth of water is suitable it is found that the salmon spawn largely on the shallows below Tehama, thus withdrawing large num bers from the propagation stations of the upper river. A careful study of the king salmon's movements on the Columbia is much to be desired. The greater length of the river, more numerous branches, and higher latitude and altitudes make that basin an extraordinary field for research, and its very great economic value demands the results.

SPAWNING STREAMS CHOSEN BY THE CO HO, DOG, AND HUMPBACK SALMON.

The coho apparently demands a yet lower temperature for spawning than the sockeye. Where it enters lake outlets early, it presses into the higher waters in much the same manner. It differs in that it often selects streams not connected with lakes, but in all cases its later arrival from the sea finds the temperature low. While the most active of any species, long journeys do not find favor with it. ' Wallowa and Baker lakes seem to be at about the limit to which it travels.

In the Naha in 1903 the cohos were spawning October 27 in a temperature of 46. This is probably about the temperature at which they begin. During October and later the small streams fall rapidly in temperature, so that scarcely any running water after that date would be too warm for spawning purposes. Since in favorable places the coho continues spawning throughout most of the winter, any temperature above freezing does not seem to be prohibitive. At Hetta it is reported that the cohos sometimes spawn in small numbers throughout the winter, even as late as March. This lake is said to have areas of open water, perhaps due to warm springs, about which sockeyes spawn until February. Alexander (ms. notes) states that in the winter of 1902-3, while the lakes and stream were frozen over, one of the lakes of South Olga stream, Kadiak Island, was visited by a party of white men and Indians who found a large number of sockeyes and cohos frozen in the ice. These were thought to be late-run fish entering after the canneries had closed. Many carcasses of salmon that had been frozen in the ice were seen by Rutter at Karluk Lake in the spring of 1903. In that stream the occurrence at times of late runs arriving after the usual closing time of the cannery early in September is well known. They more frequently occur in seasons of a small early run, and at such times the cannery is held open for them. The carcasses of winter spawners were still to bo seen on Trail Creek the last of May, 1904.

The dog and humpback salmons apparently exercise less discrimination than other species. The humpback was noted as working upstream in the Naha at 61 August 25, 1903, and in the Anan at 58 August 30, 1904; yet it had completed spawning in the outlet of Yes Lake September 11, 1905, in temperatures around 56. Karta River, September 12, 1903, was full of both dog and humpback salmon spawning at a temperature of 54, and Steelhead Creek contained many spawning humpbacks August 25, 1903, at about the same temperature. It is probable that the optimum temperature for the humpback is about the same as for the king. The dog salmon seems to accept a slightly lower degree; a few were spawning in a creek of Moira Sound as early as August 18 in 48.

NATURE OK SPAWNING BEDS SELECTED.

With the exception of the coho, the salmons appear to require a depth of water and a fineness of bed material somewhat in correspondence with their relative size. The king salmon spawns in water of a depth up to 2 or 3 feet, with a bottom of gravel and coarse sand. No exact conditions seem to be required. In the Salmon River, Idaho, the kings are reported to avoid the coarser gravel and swift currents; in the Sacramento they will spawn on bowldery rapids.

The sockeye affects shallower water for spawning than the king. On most Alaskan beds many occupy water which does not completely cover the male fish. In the selection of spawning beds this species is unique in requiring the adjacency of a lake; also it is the only species of the genus that ever spawns in still water. The lake shores chosen are more frequently portions through which a small rill flows or where seepage comes through, but sockeyes are known to spawn where no inflow of any kind is apparent.

In the streams the beds chosen are similar to those well known for various species, but, as mentioned above, in water of less depth than is usual for the king. Sometimes bottoms of fine gravel are occupied, sometimes bottoms of larger bowlders where the current is so swift as to make the holding of position precarious. No observations are recorded as to whether the first comers occupy the more accessible grounds. They apparently distribute from the beginning, and there is no evidence that a spawner ever recedes from a position once chosen and occupied. Unless carried out by the current, even the spawnedout fish remain until they die about the pool where they have spawned. At Yes Bay stream in 1903 fish could be found throughout the stream as far as the falls, but strikingly few examples were attempting to pass higher. The writer has seen no fish attempt the dam on the Naha just above the spawning beds, though cohos are said to do so. A few individuals usually enter all the small unsuitable brooks during times of freshets, apparently returning with the subsidence of the water.

In the Karluk tributaries many fish occupy beds where none of the material is of a size they can move, hence the naked eggs are swept down the current and doubtless most of them lost. In bottoms of finer material occupied by many fish dead eggs in abundance are usually to be seen in the eddies behind the hillocks formed by the spawners working up the gravel.

The coho, perhaps in its effort to reach low temperatures, frequently continues up the small streams to a point where the bottom material is coarse. In Steelhead Creek it passes humpbacks and dogs on the gravelly lower part of the stream and spawns in the rough upper portions. In all the small Alaskan streams it doubtless occupies the sockeye beds later in the season and perhaps does some damage, but the greater part of the run spawns below those beds and in creeks not entered by the sockeyes. Cohos, like the smaller species, while making their way upstream or when frightened out of the "nest," may frequently be seen in water too shallow to cover them. Whether these "nests" are excavated in shallows where the original depth is less than that of the fish, or whether the small amount of water is not more usually due to a fall in the stream subsequent to the fish's entry, has not been fully ascertained.

Humpback and dog salmon may often be seen spawning on the same beds, but in general the former is more frequently seen on finer bottoms and in shallower water, while the more powerful dog salmon sometimes occupies bottoms of coarse gravel in some depth of water. The humpback is said sometimes to fail to get beyond the reach of high tide in the selection of its spawning place.

DEPOSIT OF EGGS.

The deposit of spawn on riffles and in small streams, where it is most subject to the action of floods and frost, at first sight seems to be poor economy. But the necessities are twofold, first, aeration, and second, protection from light and enemies. In water of much depth relative to volume the bottom current is retarded, with the result that fine sediment is deposited and the circulation through the gravel or other material is impeded if not entirely cut off. If the eggs were placed in such a region of little current, they would not be carried from under the mother fish and the material for covering and protecting them would not be carried down over them, hence any such movement as the spawning fish now makes would only lead to stirring up eggs and gravel, with the result of destroying the first spawn within a few days after its deposit. For this reason the lake spawning of the sockeye must be of less proportionate value.

The action of the spawningfish in breaking away the gravel by means of forcing the body and tail against it achieves the double purpose of working the sex product down to the genital opening and of setting the fine gravel and sand in motion to cover the eggs. When first extruded the contents of the egg envelope do not quite fill it, the egg is soft and will bear considerable rough handling. Its specific gravity, only slightly greater than the water, holds it to the bottom, but allows it readily to drift along with the current. Upon finding an early lodgment the osmotic absorption of water "freezes" it to the object against which it rests, and any drifting particles of sand not heavy enough to dislodge it readily cover and conceal it from the light. It is probable that the dead eggs referred to above as seen in abundance about a well-covered ground are as often the earlier deposits dug up by later arrivals as eggs that have failed to be covered. Live eggs are almost never seen among these, as should be the case if they are of recent deposit. Uncovered eggs must eventually perish by the light even if not consumed by egg-eating fishes and birds. In ordinary currents the eggs drift perhaps but a few feet. Very early the ridge below the "nest" rises to a height that creates a bottom eddy, causing the downward motion of the eggs to cease on its lower slope. For this reason when one of these ridges is opened the greater number of eggs ordinarily is found in its lower portion.

During the season of spawning a well-covered ground becomes thrown, through the joint action of the fish and the current, into high ridges, or hillocks, sometimes as much as 2 feet above the corresponding depressions or holes. Eggs may usually be found buried in these ridges, but their semibuoyancy and spherical form make it quite difficult in a current to recover them without a screen. The abundance of dead eggs which at times collects in the eddies below these ridges has been mentioned above. On Karluk Lake in 1903, in the creek on which the spawners were counted, these beds were examined by digging in the gravel to find the condition of the deposited eggs. Between August 5 and September 2, 58 "nests" were so examined. In these were found 4,005 good eggs and 2,022 dead ones, or, in other words, about two-thirds of the buried eggs were found to be in good condition. On the latter date 587 eyed eggs were found under about 10 inches of gravel, with only 13 dead ones. This demonstrates that eggs will live and develop under proper conditions when deeply buried. In another stream, in the center of a nest, under 6 inches of gravel, only 29 of 620 eggs recovered were living. In a third bed of 1,140 eggs taken from the lower half of the nest, in a light current and from under 7 inches of gravel, only 28 were dead. In general, the observer records few eggs from locations in strong current; this was possibly in part from failure to find the eggs as well as from their scarcity. Most beds show a decided balance in favor of the good egg's. In two examinations of the connecting stream from one of the tributary lakes less than 4 per cent of the eggs were dead.

COMPLETENESS OF SPAWNING.

In 1903 a careful count was kept of the soekcyes spawning in one stream of Karluk Lake, the second from the outlet on the right or east side. This is a small creek, averaging some 10 feet in width, about 1 mile of which is used for spawning beds. From August 5 to September 5 of that year, 21,756 spawned fish were examined in this creek, presumably the total number spawning there in that time and practically the total for the season. Of these, males were in excess by about 3 per cent, the numbers being 10,723 females and 11,033 males. But one unspawned female was found dead. Dead unspawned males are more common.' Of 636 females opened, about 80 per cent were entirely spawned out, i. e., with no loose eggs in the abdominal cavity; the remaining 20 percent had an average of 97 eggs unspawned, with the most in any instance noted 1,246. The sockeye carries between 2,500 and 4,000 eggs, an average, perhaps, of about 3,500. This remnant, then, amounts to about one-half of 1 per cent of the total number of eggs matured. The product of this one stream on the same basis of estimate is 37,000,000 eggs. It is believed that less than one-tenth the number of fish entering the lake spawned in the abovementioned creek. Thus approximately 400,000,000 sockeye eggs were spawned in Karluk Lake basin in 1903. Sockeyea are reported by natives to spawn late in the winter, even under the ice, but it is doubtful whether it is usual for any noteworthy number to occur as a fall run, as with other species and in more southerly streams.

In 1903 the spawning season was practically over early in September. Since the fishing continues ordinarily into that month, the spawning should last much later. The double operation of cannery and hatchery, perhaps, accounts for its early close. On the Naha the season continues into November. At Hetta the flsh are reported to spawn in small numbers until later in the winter.

PERCENTAGE OF NATURAL PRODUCTION.

The percentage of natural production of fry is a matter of the utmost interest. In daylight observation of a well-populated spawning ground one is sometimes struck *by* the absence of factors to cause damage. At Yes Bay, Karta Bay, Kegan, the Naha, Wards Cove, and other places one may see hundreds of various species spawning uninterruptedly. At times on the humpback beds where fish are numerous the dead eggs lie in numbers in the eddies for days and even weeks untouched, not a trout or sculpin in sight—though it is certain that at least a few are in protected places near by. The ducks arrive late after most of the spawning in that region is over. It is believed by the writer that the natural loss of spawn has been overestimated.

In Steelhead Creek in 1903 comparatively few cohos were noted— it is believed not more than 50 pairs; yet over 3,000 fry of that species were sometimes taken in a single night as they were leaving for the sea. The run begins early in May and lasts until July. In six sets of the net in May ami June an average of about 1,300 of these fry were taken, which indicates a run of between 50,000 and 75,000 for the season, or a product of at least 30 per cent. Similar facts regarding steelheads were noted in the same creek, which was observed carefully in both 1903 and 1904 for spawning steelheads in an effort to take sufficient eggs for an experiment. Not over a dozen pairs could be seen either season, yet early in July the fry were migrating at the rate of 200 to 300 per night and the creek was full of them till the fall rains swept them out.

Regarding the migration of sockeye young from Seton Lake in 1903, Babcock states: "The sight was amazing, and impressed one with the fact that the percentage of natural fertilization of ova and the survival of the resulting fry was greater than has been generally believed by the authorities."

It will be noted that eyed eggs were found in the Karluk creeks on September 2. On this date the lake surface was 44, having fallen about 10 in as many days. With the shortening of the days and prevalent cloudy weather the temperatures must fall rapidly from this date, and it is questionable whether any but the earliest deposited and hence most advanced eggs hatch before the onset of freezing weather.

Fry were found as late as August 1 in the stream just below the lake; species unidentified. It is improbable that any considerable number of sockeye eggs hatch in time for the young to seek the shelter of the lake for the winter. With the congealing of the waters in the mountains the streams will become reduced in volume and the entire bed must at times become frozen over, part by its exposure and the remainder by the formation of anchor ice. The habit of the flsh of spawning on the shallow riffles must unfailingly subject the spawn to this influence. That it is not an exterminating influence is due to the covering of gravel which the eggs have received. The depth to which the bared beds freeze in winter has not been ascertained. At points where a constant current percolates through, such as must occur on the spawning riffles, it is improbable that this depth is so great as might be suspected in view of the low air temperatures.

The effects of freshets are largely nullified by the season at which they occur. Late fall rains produce comparatively small floods for the reason that the precipitation in the hills falls as snow. The spring floods which come with the melting snows will find the eggs in great part hatched, and fry are largely able to rise above the deposit.

RELATION OF SPAWNING HABITS TO NUMBER OF FISH.

The spawning habits of a species bear a suggestive relation to its abundance. The humpback in Southeast Alaska far outnumbers all others. This is a region of small streams, and practically all that have a suitable bed and are accessible from the sea are utilized by this salmon. The small size of the adult humpback makes spawning possible in even shallower water than the sockeye or coho requires. The number of eggs, about 2,000, is perhaps less than in other species. The incubation period is less than that of the sockeye or king. This, with the early arrival on the beds and consequent high temperature of the incubating water, brings the humpback egg to a hardy stage early in the season and the fry to a stage of development that sends them seaward with the opening of spring. The small size and light color of the egg also may be advantageous. In regions of larger rivers, such as Bristol Bay, the number of humpbacks is much less in proportion to other species. The same is true for more southerly regions. In the Bristol Bay region the average size of humpbacks is considerably less than in Southeast Alaska. Whether these facts are due to the character of the streams can only be surmised.

The limited number of cohos ccn not be attributed to scarcity of spawning beds of the nature required. These are scarcely less widely distributed than those suitable for the humpback. The spawn incubates in about the same time, but is somewhat larger and more brightly colored. The increased number of eggs, about 3,000, should offset the disadvantage of size. The cohos coming last to the beds, their eggs are undisturbed by other fishes, but since much of the spawning is late the loss from physical causes may be greater. The fry are probably less active, reach the sea later in the season, and perhaps suffer greater loss from predatory enemies.

The dog salmon, while widely scattered, occurs in numbers only in selected streams. The eggs are very large, rather light colored, and run about 3,000 to the fish. The incubation period probably differs little from that of the humpback. The fry reach the sea early, and there is no obvious reason why this should be one of the scarcer species.

The spawning habits of both king and sockeye are obviously advantageous. The king, resorting to large rivers, is able, by its strength to reach waters where the conditions are most favorable. Other species do not work over its beds; and though limited in the main trunks entered, the king secures extent of territory in the numerous branches; the habits of the young permit them to obtain the necessary food in the streams, and the distance of the trip to be performed insures their sufficient age and size for adequate protection upon reaching the sea and its rapacious inhabitants. The summer residence conserves the species to an extent, while the migration of the main body as fry prevents overpopulation of the limited freshwater area. In this connection it is of interest to note that the fish found in the Columbia headwaters in 1895 were of less than the average size for that stream, weighing only 10 to 14 pounds. Even allowing for tissue expenditure during the ascent of the stream this does not indicate that the stronger fish travel farthest, but rather the contrary. It seems possible that at a certain point the beds are occupied by the stronger fish and that the less powerful go beyond in search of unpreempted grounds.

The sockeye profits by its lake habit. An unoccupied food supply is thus made available, and protection for the immature young is obtained in waters not naturally inhabited by many predaceous animals. In basins of large productiveness the overflow of fry, migrating as such, conserves the lake food suppl'. In the main the species secures immunity from disturbance on the spawning beds, passing beyond all but coho and king and avoiding the latter by selection of colder water.

CHANGES INCIDENT TO MATURATION.

The changes that are associated with maturation of the reproductive element vary in extent in the sexes, in the species, and with the age. The production of the jaws and growth of canine teeth that is more or less characteristic of all male salmons is seen also in the trout and the charr. The change in body form—the increase in depth by the ridging of the back—is much more developed in the salmon. The changes seem to be greater in the larger, and presumably older, fish. The grilse of the king show very little of it, scarcely more than the female, and in the case of fingerlings in the Sacramento which develop mature spermatozoa there is no evident external change.

In the trout and charr the upper jaw elongates somewhat but does not become hooked. The lower jaw elongates and becomes knobbed or hooked; this swelling is usually received in a corresponding recess or notch in the upper jaw, but sometimes is sufficiently large to prevent complete closure of the mouth. After the spawning season is over these growths are to an extent resorbed, but the jaws never fully recover their original shape.

In the Sacramento the king salmon of the spring run show none of these characters until some time after entering the fresh water. The late runs, being more developed, show some changes by the time they have reached the mouth of the river in Suisun Bay. The various changes, which have been fully described by Rutter, are progressive with the development of the reproductive elements. Little of the red color is shown by this species except in the large (old?) males, and even in these never approaches the brilliancy of the sockeye or coho. Neither do they as fully develop the body depth as species which frequent shallower waters.

The Alaskan sockeye at the time it is first taken in the fisheries has already begun to show the hooked jaw, so that with care one can distinguish the sexes in the larger fish. Cases will occur, however, in which the female has jaws somewhat prolonged, and there are corresponding cases of males with neat heads, so that in statistical work it is essential that the fish be opened to make sure of the sex. Late in the season, or in occasional schools at any time, the males are more readily distinguishable.

When the sockeyes emerge from the lake en route to the spawning beds the change has become complete. The entire fish, except the head and fins, has changed from its original green and silver to a brilliant vermilion or maroon. The head retains its bright green color and the fins become variously dark. At this time the sockeye rivals the tropical fishes in beauty of coloration. The elongation of jaws and development of depth are extreme in large males; the females show little of it and acquire less brilliance of color, in some cases scarcely any.

The grilse (Arctic salmon) exhibit less change than the large fish, but show all the characters to a degree.

The dwarf sockeye exhibits very little change; sex of ripe fish taken in Wallowa Lake can not be distinguished by external appearance. At the time of entering streams for spawning they are thus described by Kendall:

Back olive green, more or less spotted with black; dorsal and caudal somewhat spotted; sides dusky metallic blue or smoky with faint marks like parr marks; belly white or slightly dusky. Pectorals, ventrals, and anal black, tipped with white; outer ray of pectorals white; a general brassy luster after the fish has been out of water some time.

Colors, spotting, etc., vary in different individuals, but there is never any red. In Alturas Lake in larger examples of the dwarf the red is sometimes present and the other changes are somewhat more marked.

The coho shows more change in the female than any other species, and the jaw develops more knob, as in the trout. It is sometimes difficult to distinguish the sexes among spawning fishes in the Naha. Both may acquire a red almost as brilliant as the sockeye's, so that in the water it is easy to mistake either species for the other.

The extreme height of the back in the male of the humpback and the characteristic color blotching of it and of the dog salmon are well known. The females of the two species, particularly the latter, retain silvery colors and neat forms more full' than other species.

The useful purpose, if any, which these changes subserve is difficult to surmise. It may easily be believed that the development of teeth, and of jaws to render them effective, is a matter of defense with the male. It does not hesitate to make use of the weapon to drive away intruders, but its awkward and slow movements render its armature of no avail so far as trout and other egg-eating fish are concerned. The only service is in preventing other males of the same species from mating with the female, and even in this the ability is not always equal to the emergency. A small active male has been seen to slip alongside a spawning female during the absence of her consort in pursuit of another interloper and administer all the attention shown by her regular attendant. In general it may be assumed that in this manner nature secures the offspring of the well-developed mature males, which offspring is known to be stronger and more thrifty than that of the younger fish.

The exhibition of beauty in color and form in the male, which has been thought to be the result of sex selection, can hardly be so considered in the case of these fish. The female apparently has no option in the matter. The larger male will drive away the smaller and take possession. The peculiar compression of the male, with the flattening of the ventral aspect, increases its ability to work through the shallow water, which the small size of the female, without such change, allows it to enter.

RETURN OF ADULTS TO SALT WATER.

To test the question of the return of salmon to salt water after once entering a river system, Rutter, in 1903, made two experiments. Eight hundred salmon (species not noted, but probably mainly if not all sockeyes) were tagged and released in Karluk Lagoon (brackish water) 1 mile from the sea. Four hundred of these were released June 12 and 15. One was retaken outside in a cannery seine 1 hour after release, 3 were retaken entering Karluk Lake after 11, 13, and 34 days, respectively; 2 were retaken by seines in the lagoon, and 1 died in the lagoon. Doubtless many of the tags were lost, and perhaps many fish. entered the lakes or were retaken outside and unobserved.

Five hundred and fourteen were tagged and released on June 30. One of these was retaken in New Red (Ayakulik) River, 40 miles down the coast, 3 days later. One reached the lake in 10 days; another was found spawning there August 2; one was seined in the lagoon 2 days after release; and another, a green female somewhat fungused and worn, 27 days after. No others were reported.

This experiment is very incomplete and most desirable data are lacking, especially as to whether the fish were taken into the lagoon in a live car or were seined in the lagoon after voluntary entrance. The influence of the tag, clamped to the lower jaw by a strong ring, in irritating the fish and stimulating unnatural action can not be estimated. The results point to the probability that some fish remain in the lagoon for several days, some reenter the ocean, and others spend varying times somewhere between the lagoon and lake.

Another experiment was the tagging of 255 individuals at the mouth of the lake, from July 3 to 25. Of these, 123 were males, 64 of which were ripe and 66 showing more or less of decay, fungus, etc; 132 were females, 23 ripe, and 70 in poor condition. These fish were "taken in a trap built at the outlet of the lake, but on the shallow or small current side. This location unfortunately led to the securing of a large percentage of weak fish, and made the results less valuable. In general, fish reach the lakes in sound condition. Of these tagged fish, 3 females and 1 male were retaken in the ocean by the cannery seines in from three to eleven days after tagging, 1 was retaken in the trap the following day, and 2 males were found in the spawning creeks.

The main interest attaching to this result is in the number of ripe fish obtained at the entrance to the lake. The percentage of ripe fish in the number trapped is of no point, since the strong green fish entered in the heavy current beyond the trap. It may be that these fish were hindered from making an early ascent of the river by the seining carried on for the cannery, and that such a condition of ripeness is unnatural. If there is no purpose in a lake residence of about one month it is difficult to see how it should have been brought to be the normal habit. That these exceptions were abnormalities is shown by the failure to find any of these tagged fish in the nearly 22,000 spawned fish examined at a creek which these ripe fish would most naturally seek, the nearest good ground about the lake.

The main body of fish entering Karluk Lake came in against the stronger current and in the deeper water. During the clay they entered in small schools of 20 to 60 or more, at intervals of a minute or less. They seemed to linger about the foot of the lake some days.

ENEMIES OF YOUNG SALMON.

In the trap at the mouth of Karluk Lake in 1903, 190 charrs were taken between June 5 and July 25. The biggest catch (20) was made on June 5, after which the number fell off rapidly. The next highest catch was made June 26, about ten days after the arrival of the first salmon. On the 27th a charr of 535 mm. length was taken with salmon eggs in its stomach. On July 1 a steelhead, also containing salmon eggs, was taken. One hundred and fifty-seven, or about 82 per cent, of the stomachs were empty; 14, or 7% per cent, contained remains of fish, mostly cottoids; 13, or 7 per cent, contained insects or their larvae; 6, or over 3 per cent, contained mollusks, snails, and clams; 3 in addition had eaten eggs, 2 salmon eggs, and the third those of some small fish.

It will be observed that these fish were taken in an "upstream" trap into which the fish would come from the river. In the river at this time were numerous schools of salmon fry and small fingerlings, yet there is no record that any stomach contained a single identifiable young salmon.

During May and June many of these trout (?) were seen jumping near the foot of the lake. On the first day the trap was installed, May 29, 10 were taken; on the 31st, 9, etc. No young salmon are reported in these. Upon the occupation of the spawning beds by the salmon the trout follow to feed on their spawn. This probably forms a large part of their food until late in the season, when the maggots from the flies breeding in the dead salmon become more common. On August 19, 131 charrs were taken in a seine haul in a spawning creek. One hundred and twenty-eight of these were feeding on maggots; 3 contained insects, and 1 a cottoid; 54 were without salmon eggs; but the remaining 77 contained from 1 to 110 eggs each, an average of 16. At this time there were few live spawning salmon in the creek, and few dead eggs in sight in the eddies, where earlier there had been an abundance. The trout were more numerous than at any previous time, in schools of 30 to 50 as well as many isolated individuals.

In the salt water about Karluk Beach they were even more abundant than in the lake. Sometimes as many as 2,000 are taken in a single haul, and ordinarily at least 500. No effort is made to destroy them. July 20, 220 of these were examined for stomach contents. The most common food was small crustaceans of several species, next in abundance sand launces, both adult and half grown being quite common; young cod were found in many, 40 being taken from one stomach. No other fish were found. July 25, of 22 examples, 7 to 18 inches in length, from the hatchery corral (fresh water), 17 were feeding; 2 had salmon eggs, 1 had 5 2-inch salmon fingerlings, others had various crustaceans. Of 19 examples, 10 to 20 inches in length, from the lagoon, examined July 28, only 4 were feeding. One had eggs, 1 maggots, 1 young sand launces, and the other some unidentifiable fish. No rainbow or cutthroat trout were seen in Karluk Lake.

July 14, 1903, the stomachs of 28 rainbow trout, 2 cutthroat, and 2 charrs, taken in the Naha, were examined. None contained young salmon; 1 contained small eggs like herring eggs, and all the rest contained only caddis larva-. The fish ranged from 2 feet to about 8 inches in length. At that time of year many coho young are resident in the river.

During the summer of 1905 many trout of the three species from Yes River were examined. No record was kept of the number, but it amounts to at least a hundred. In these the food was mainly caddis and insects from the surface. No young salmon were found, though coho young were present in the stream.

Trout and charrs have been taken near the hatchery at the head of Heckman Lake with numbers of fry in their stomachs. The exact conditions are not known. In the planting of large numbers of fry or small fingerlings, some are sure to be at least for a time cUsabled and numbers can readily be captured by an active fish. The loss is apt to be especially large if the plant is made in a vicinity where bad eggs have been dumped, and the waters thus "baited."

The sculpin or bullhead would seem to be a more dangerous enemy to the salmon fry than is the trout. It lurks under the stones in just such places as the fry will seek for shelter. Its movements are extremely rapid and its appetite insatiable.

Ducks are perhaps the most active enemy of the salmon in Alaska, especially the sawbill *(Merganser)* and golden eye *(Clangulu)*. All ducks will doubtless root up the beds in low water, but those just mentioned, as well as the harlequin *(Histrionicus)* and the gulls and terns, will dive for eggs. The sawbill is resident in Southeast Alaska, where the young arrive in time to feed on the coho fry but rather too late for others. In the fall the birds work with the spawning salmon, diving for the eggs as they are extruded or exposed by the shifting of the gravel. Mallards feed more on the blowfly maggots in the dead fish, but apparently find a sufficient number of eggs to ruin the flavor of their flesh for the table. The larger flocks of ducks arrive rather late in the season in the Loring district, doing greatest damage to the coho in large streams, but a considerable number arrive in time for the earlier species of salmon. The-do not seem to frequent the small streams, except those tributary to lakes. The grebe family does not seem ordinarily to take young salmon.

GEOGRAPHICAL GLOSSARY.

Following is a list of the geographical names used in this report, with approximate position of the places. The astronomical position is given of rivers and bays for their mouths, of islands for the center, of straits for the center or the more prominent mouth or connecting end. *Admiralty Inlet,* waters between Whidby Island and the mainland to the westward. 48 N., 122 40'W.
Alder Creek, one of two main tributaries entering at the head of upper Karta Lake. *Alert Bay,* small bight on south side of Cormorant Island north of Vancouver Island 50 35' N., 126 57' W.
Aleutian Islands, chain of islands on the south of Bering Sea. *Alturas Lake,* small lake of the Columbia Basin, tributary to Salmon River, central
Idaho. 43 55' N., 114 51' W. *Anan Stream,* stream emptying into Bradfield Canal from the south. 50 12' N., 131 49' W.
Annette Island, small island south of Revillagigedo Island. 55 08'N., 131 30' W. *Bard, V. S.* hatchery on the McCloud River, northern California. *Baker Lake,* small lake in northern Washington, tributary to the Skagit River. Location of United States hatchery. 4844' N., 121 37' W. *Bartlett Bay,* small bight off east side of Glacier Bay. 58 27' N., 135 53' W. *Battle Creek,* tributary of the Sacramento River, northern California. *Behm Canal,* channel separating Revillagige-

do Island from Cleveland Peninsula on the west and the mainland on the east.
Bering Island, largest of the Komandorski group. *Bora de Quadra,* long, narrow fiord in the mainland south of Revillagigedo Island. 55 0y N., 131 W.
Bradfield Canal, deep fiord in the mainland above Cleveland Peninsula. 55 11' N., 132 W. *Bristol Bay,* large bay north of Alaska Peninsula. 58 N., 159 W.
Cape Caamano, south point of Cleveland Peninsula. 55 *30* N., 131 58' W.
Cape Chacon, south point of Prince of Wales Island. 54 42' N., 132 01' W.
Carroll Inlet, long, narrow inlet in southern part of Revillagigedo Island. 55 20' N.,
131 128' W.
Chinook River, small tributary of the Columbia near its mouth. 46 18' N., 123 58' W. *Clackamas River,* tributary of the Willamette, Oregon;.site of United States hatchery. *Clarence Strait,* main channel east of Prince of Wales Island.
Cleveland Passage, small strait separated from east sideof Frederick Sound by Whitney
Island. 57 14' N., 133 30' W. *Cleveland Peninsula,* extension of the mainland northwest of Revillagigedo Island, 55 45' N., 132 W. *Columbia River,* large river between Washington and Oregon.
Deep lMoser) Bay, small bight on west side of Revillagigedo Island below Naha Bay. 55 34' N., 131 3 W. *Dixon Entrance,* waters between Queen Charlotte Islands and Alaska. 54 3IK X., 133 W.
Dolomi, village on east side of Prince of Wales Island just north of Moira Sound. 55 08' N., 132' 03'W. *Dorr Falh,* falls on the Naha above Roosevelt Lagoon. See map. *Dundas Bay,* small bay off Cross Sound to the northward. 58 25' N. , 136 12' W. *Emma Creek,* small creek falling into Jordan Lake. See map. *Ernest Sound,* waters northwest of Cleveland Peninsula, opening into Clarence Strait. 55 5C N., 132 15' W. *Flume Creek,* small creek near Loring. See map. *Forlmann Hatchery,* Alaska Packers' Association hatchery on Heckman Lake. See map. *Fraser River,* largest river of British Columbia. 49 06' N., 123 08' W.
Gibson Creek, small creek falling into Jordan Lake. See map.
Harvester Island, island in mouth of LTyak Bay. Kodiak Island.
Heckman Lake, second fresh-water lake of the Xaha system. See map.
Helm Bay Creek, stream in southern part of Cleveland Peninsula. 55 38' N., 131 58' W.
Helta, an inlet, lake, and stream on west side of Prince of Wales Island. 55 08' X.,
132 31i' W.
Hirsch Rapids, tidal rapids at head of Naha Bay. See map. *Humboldt Harbor,* small bight on west side of Popof Island, Shumagin group. 55 2C N., 1(0 32' W. *Isanotski Strait,* water separating Unimak Island from Alaska Peninsula. 54 53' N., 163 23' W. *Jordan Lake,* first fresh-water lake of the Xaha system. See map. *Juan de Fuca Strait,* waters between Vancouver Island and Washington, connecting
Puget Sound with the Pacific Ocean. 48 30' X., 124 40' W. *Juneau,* town on mainland, northern part of Southeast Alaska. 58 18' N., 134 24' W. *Karluk,* village on west side Kodiak Island. 57 35' N., 154 18' W. The bay, lagoon, river, and lake adjacent of same name.
Karta Bay, small bight at head of Kasaan Bay. 55 35' N., 132 34' W. River and lakes of same name.
Kasaan Bay, inlet on east side of Prince of Wales Island. 55 25' N., 132 10' W.
Kegan, small stream, lake, and bight opening into Moira Sound. 55 01' N. , 132 10' W. *Ketchikan Creek,* small stream on west side of Revillagigedo Island, falling into Tongasa
Narrows. 55 21' N., 131 38' W. Town of same name. *Kilisut Harbor,* long, narrow, shallow inlet opposite town of Port Townsend, Wash.
48 04' N., 122 43' W. *Killisnoo,* village on west side of Admiralty Island. 57 28' N., 134 34' W. *Kiska Island,* one of the Aleutian Islands. 52 N., 178 30' W. *Klauak,* village, stream, and lake on west side Prince of Wales Island. 55 33' N., 133 07' W. *Kodiak,* village on east side of Kodiak Island. 57 48' N.. 152 24' W. *Kodiak Island,* large island on west side of the Gulf of Alaska. 57 30' N., 153 30' W. *Komandorskis,* group of
islands east of Kamchatka. 55 N., 174 W. *Kiichak River,* main stream at the head of Bristol Bay. 58 55' N., 157 W.
Lake Creek, the outlt't of Seaton Lake, Brit ish Columbia. *Larsen Cove* (or Bay), bight off west side of Uyak Bay. 57 33' N., 153 53' W. *Loring,* village on Naha Bay, Revillagigedo Island. 55 36' N., 131 38' W. See map. *Lytton,* town of British Columbia at the junction of the Thompson with the Fraser. *Mare Island,* island in north part of San Pablo Bay, California. 38 04' N., 122 1G' W.
McCloud River, tributary of the Sacramento (Pit) in northern California. 40 45' N., 122 20' W. *McCune Creek,* small stream falling into head of Heckman Lake. See map. *Mellakatla,* village on west side of Annette Island. 5508' N. , 131 34' W. *Moira Sound,* branching inlet on east side of southern end of Prince of Wales Island. 55 05' N., 132 W. *Monterey Bay,* bay in central part of California coast. 36 45' N., 122 W.
Naha Bay, bight on west aide of Revillagigedo Island. 55 36' N., 131 40' W. River of same name. *New Morzhovoi,* village on east side Isanotski Strait. 54 54' N., Ki3 18' W.
New Red lAyakulik) River, stream of the southwestern part of Kodiak Island. 57 11'
N., 154 30' W.
Nichols Passage, water west of Annette Island, between Clarence Strait and Tongase
Narrows.
Nicolai's barabara, an old barabara in Karluk River below the lake.
Nikolski, anchorage at Bering Island.
North Arm, northern arm of Moira Sound. 55 05' N., 132 04' W.
Nowiskay, lake and stream emptying into North Arm. 55 07' N., 132 08' W.
Oakland, city on San Francisco Bay, California.
Old Johnson, lake and stream emptying into Moira Sound from the south. 54 5!K N., 132 Ofi' W. *Oaten Creek,* main stream at head of Quadra Lake. *Otter Bay,* small bight on west side of Pender Island. 48 48' N., 123 18' W. *Otter Point,* projection of Vancouver Island into Juan de Fuca Strait. 48 21' N., 123 4 W. *Ozette Lake,* small lake in north-

western part of Washington. 48 05' N. , 124 40' W. *Papermill Creek,* small creek tributary to Tomales Bay, California, just above San Francisco. 38 10' N., 122 50' W. *Patching Lake,* third fresh-water lake of the Naha system. See map. *Pavlof Harbor,* small bight off Freshwater Bay, Chicago!' Island, Southeast Alaska. 57 41' N., 135 01' W. *Payette River,* tributary' of the Snake River in western Idaho. 44 05' N., 116 58' W. *Pender Island,* small island north of Haro Strait. 48 47' N., 123 16' W. *Peninsula of Alaska,* the long peninsula in the southwest of Alaska. *Point Adams,* point of Prince of Wales Island north of Moira Sound. 55 07' N., 132 W. *Point Wggins,* westernmost point of Revillagigedo Island. 55 27' N., 131 50' W. *Port Alexander,* bay on east side Nigei Island, southern part of Queen Charlotte Sound. 50 50'N., 127 40'W. *Port Clester,* bay indenting Annette Island on the west. *Prince of Wales Island,* largest island of Alexander Archipelago, Southeast Alaska. 55 30' N., 133 W. *Puget Soutul,* large sound in northwestern Washington.
Quadra. (See Boca de Quadra.)
Quesncl Dam, a point on the Fraser River.
Revillagigedo Island, large island in the southern part of Alexander Archipelago. 55 30'N., 131 30'W. *Rivers Inlet,* inlet of British Columbia, south end of Hecate Strait. 51 26' N., 127 40' W. *Roosevelt Lagoon,* body of brackish water at mouth of the Naha River. See map. 10731—07 8 *Sacramento,* river and city of California.
Salmon River, tributary of Snake River, western Idaho. 45 50' N., 116 *W W.*
San Pablo Bay, bay above San Francisco Bay. 38 05' N., 122 23' W.
Seton Lake, large lake of the Fraser system, British Columbia.
Shelikqf Strait, waters between Kodiak Island and Alaska Peninsula.
Shelter Island, island at the head of Stephens Passage. 58 26' N., 134 51' W.
Sherringham Point, projection of Vancouver Island into Strait of Juan de Fuca. 48 23'N., 123 55'W.
Shumagin Islands, group south of Alaska Peninsula. 55 N., 160 W.
South Olga Stream, stream entering southern end of Olga Bay, southern part of Kodiak
Island. 57 06' N., 154 20' W.
Spacious Bay, bay on east side of neck of Cleveland Peninsula. 5551'N., 131 46' W.
Steelhead Creek, small creek falling into Naha Bay. See map.
StiHne River, large river from mainland in Southeast Alaska. 55 36' N., 132 22' W.
Sucia Islands, small group just south of Georgia Strait. 48 46' N., 122 54' W.
Suisun Bay, bay above San Pablo Bay, receiving the Sacramento River. 38 07' N.,
122 W.
Sumner Harbor 1Bay), small bay northeast of town of Unalaska. 53 54' N., 166 27' W.
Susquehanna River, river in eastern Pennsylvania.
Tamgas, inlet in the southern part of Annette Island. 53 01' N., 131 32' W.
Tehama, town on the Sacramento River, California, near head of steamboat navigation.
Thompson River, tributary of the Fraser from the east, in British Columbia. 50 03' X., 120 10'W.
Thome Bay. small inlet on east side of Prince of Wales Island, north of Kasaan Bay. 5540/ N., 132 27' W.
Tongass Narrows, teach on southwest side of Revillagigedo Island connecting Behm
Canal with Revillagigedo channel.
Trail Creek, small creek connecting Trout Ponds with Roosevelt Lagoon. See map.
Tribune Bay, small bight on south side of Hornby Island. 49 31' N., 124 38' W.
Trocadero, aquarium at Paris, France.
Trout Ponds, two small lakes near Loring. See map.
Ugaguk, large stream falling into Bristol Bay from the'east. 58 14' N., 157 34' W.
Uganuk, bay in the north side of Kodiak Island. 57 54' N., 153 30' W.
Umnak Island, one of the Aleutian Islands, lying about 53 15' N., 168 15' W.
Unalaska, town on the north side of Unalaska Island. 53 52' N., 166 32' W.
Union Bay, small bight off Baynes Sound, east side of Vancouver Island. 49 35' N.,
124 54' W.
Unuk Hirer, large river falling into Burroughs Bay at head of Revillagigedo Island.
56 03' N., 131 07' W.
Uyak Bay, deep inlet on west side of Kodiak Island. 57 45' N., 153 53' W.
Wallowa River, river in northeastern Oregon, tributary to the Grande Ronde. 46 03'
N., 40 03' W.
Walnut Grove, village on the Sacramento River, between Sacramento and Suisun Bay.
Wannuk River, tributary of Rivers Inlet, British Columbia.
Ward Cove, small bay on west side of Revillagigedo Island, between Point Higgins and
Ketchikan.
Whidby Island, large island in the northern part of Puget Sound. 48 09' N., 122 34' W.
Willamette River, large river of western Oregon, tributary to the Columbia.
Willow Creek, one of two main tributaries entering head of upper Karta Lake.
Wood River, large river emptying into Bristol Bay from the north. 59 N., 158 23' W.
Wrangell, town in north end of W'rangell Island. 56 28' N., 132 22' W.
Yes Bay, narrow inlet on east side of neck of Cleveland Peninsula opening into Behm
Canal. 5o 53' N., 131 42' W. Lake and stream of same name. Site of United
States hatchery
o
Plate IV.
Plate V.

CPSIA information can be obtained at www.ICGtesting.com
Printed in the USA
BVOW06s1041160215

387914BV00017B/290/P